ID0984633

THE ANATOMY OF LANGUAGE

SAYING WHAT WE MEAN

THE
ANATOMY OF LANGUAGE

SAYING WHAT WE MEAN

by

MARJORIE BOULTON
M.H., B.Litt.

ROUTLEDGE & KEGAN PAUL LTD
Broadway House, 68–74 Carter Lane
London

First published in 1959
by Routledge & Kegan Paul Limited
Broadway House, 68-74 Carter Lane
London, EC4V 5EL
Second impression 1968
Third impression 1971
Printed in Great Britain
by Eyre and Spottiswoode Limited at Grosvenor Press
Portsmouth

ISBN 0 7100 6288 5 (c)
ISBN 0 7100 6351 2 (p)

To

IVO LAPENNA
a master of words
who has given me a better understanding
of the meaning of such words as *courage,*
loyalty, honour and *friendship*

CONTENTS

Contents

PART III

Literary Semantics

FOREWORD

MY purpose in writing this small book was to stimulate a thoughtful, critical and socially useful interest in the meaning of words. I have tried to relate problems of elementary semantics to everyday human problems. As I have written the book mainly for older schoolchildren and students, I have tried to choose, as far as possible, examples that may be relevant to their urgent concerns; thinking of a school audience, I have also made a few concessions to conventionality, for which I beg pardon. I hope the book may also be helpful to older people who are interested in language but have no specialized knowledge in this field of study.

My book is a mere popularization of what can be a highly academic subject. This is fully intentional: formal and scholarly studies of semantics can be inexhaustibly fascinating to a minority; but I have written for people who will never read such studies. The quest for truth and integrity is not confined to philosophers and lexicographers; it is a true lifetime cause fit for many a young rebel; and our sense of the meaning of words touches our private lives very nearly.

I am deeply grateful to Professor W. E. Collinson for checking the chapter on International Semantics. I am also grateful to all the unintentional contributors of examples.

I believe I have made no discoveries in semantics, but have merely made some old knowledge rather more accessible and digestible; yet I dare to hope that this little book may provoke

thought and perhaps, here and there, make some small contribution to human happiness.

M. B.

Stoke-on-Trent,
October 1958.

PART I

Understanding and Misunderstanding

I. WHAT ARE WORDS FOR?

MAN is the only creature that uses words intentionally and habitually. A parrot or a mynah may
talk in a fashion, but it would be impossible
to discuss any subject with a talking bird. We use words
in order to tell somebody something, that is, to communicate.

Speech and writing are not essential to human life; deaf
and dumb people and idiots who cannot learn to speak may
live if their bodily necessities are provided and may even, it
seems, enjoy some satisfactions; but all human beings who
are able to do so speak sometimes. Indeed, for most of us
prolonged silence is distressing. 'I shall never speak to you
again!' is regarded as a serious threat, a mark of the most
extreme displeasure; and some ascetics regard silence as one
of their mortifications. We all seem to have a natural wish
to communicate with other people.

We may wish to communicate various kinds of information, for example:

Facts. 'The train will leave from platform four at 11.20.
There will be a restaurant car in the rear of the train. The two
front coaches are reserved for passengers joining the train at
Doncaster.'

Commands or perhaps wishes. This time we do not merely
tell someone something; we try to make the person to whom
we speak do something, or perhaps we express our desires
that no one can satisfy:

'Bring me a glass of water.' 'Hold that prop there and don't

3

move!' 'I wish I had masses of wavy raven hair, liquid dark eyes and long eyelashes!'

Emotions. 'I do so love you. You are wonderful. You are everything in the world to me.' 'You make me sick! I can't bear the sight of you!' 'I've won the marmalade competition, oh joy, joy! joy! Hooroo! Oh glorious day, peal all the bells, bless all the peel!'

Arguments. 'If the world is really a flat disc, as you say, why is there no record that anyone has ever fallen off the edge?'

Sociable noises. A good many words we use mean hardly anything except that they are conventionally taken as implying that we are fairly well disposed to the person addressed and wish to remain on good terms with him or her. For example, to reply to the question 'How do you do?' with a detailed account of our last medical examination is not at all what is expected. 'Excuse me!' 'I beg your pardon!' 'Please . . .', 'Don't mention it . . .' are examples of such sociable noises. Often when people talk about topics in which they feel no real interest such a statement as 'It's a fine day!' or 'This train is very slow!' is not so much a comment on the weather or on the speed of the train as a noise meant to suggest that the speaker wishes to be civil and sociable.

If someone sees me looking about the table, guesses my need correctly and passes me the salt, I am likely to say 'Thank you very much.' There is a great deal of difference between such a 'Thank you very much', which is more a piece of normal politeness than the expression of an emotion, and 'I am most grateful. . . . I shall never forget your kindness!' which is the kind of expression we use when someone has done a real favour, important to our welfare and probably requiring some trouble or sacrifice.

Magic. In primitive communities the idea that words have magic properties is still very much alive. Today in England it is found mostly in a few taboos: for example, some people show a degree of horror at certain swear-words which is out of all proportion to their literal meaning; children are sometimes afraid of particular words and will not even pronounce them. Ignorant or naïve people sometimes mix up the idea of prayer with the idea of magic. Primitive people often repeat certain words to make the crops grow, to kill their enemies and so on, and believe that to know a person's name is to have power over them. (And why is it common even today, for a hostile person in anger to address the enemy by the full name instead of the first name or surname as is usual?) Are magic words communication? Perhaps in a sense they are communication with supernatural powers.

voodoo is religion not magic

Enquiry. We may use words not to communicate actual information, opinions or emotion, but to communicate our own desire to know something. 'Can you tell me the way to the cathedral?' 'What do you think of Phil Mugg?' 'Are you upset about something?'

Pure joy in words. People with a fair command of words very often enjoy using them, and practise what we might call redundant communication for the fun of saying things as elaborately and eloquently as possible. For example, in Shakespeare's *Henry IV*, part 1, the Prince wishes to say that Falstaff is much too fat and Falstaff wishes to say that the Prince is ridiculously thin; but their essentially repetitive, yet delightfully varied, invective is much more amusing than a simple statement of weight would be:

> *Prince:* . . . this sanguine coward, this bed-presser, this horseback-breaker, this huge hill of flesh;
> *Falstaff:* 'Sblood, you starveling, you elf-skin, you dried neat's tongue, you bull's pizzle, you stock-fish! O! for breath to utter what is like thee; you tailor's yard, you sheath, you bow-case, you vile standing tuck;
>
> (Act II, scene iv.)

B

What are Words For?

Very often we cannot classify the reasons for using words exactly; for example, it is not always easy to sort out the precise proportions of fact, emotion, opinion and wish in a remark.

What happens when we speak without any audience? We are still, in a sense, communicating, for we are communicating with ourselves, telling ourselves to do something, encouraging ourselves, telling ourselves agreeable stories about ourselves (day-dreams), and formulating our emotions. Most people know that to put our emotions into words, even in complete solitude, usually makes it easier to deal with them. We may even talk to ourselves with the specific purpose of communicating with a part of our mind not fully under our own control. This is auto-suggestion—intentional auto-suggestion. It is a better instrument than an alarm-clock for getting up at a particular hour; for instance, to say to oneself firmly several times, just before going to bed and in bed, 'I shall get up at six o'clock' is a fairly good way of being certain to do so; and similar auto-suggestive tricks can improve our health and help in various fields of activity. So though we appear not to be communicating when we talk to ourselves, we may in fact be conversing with our 'other selves'—an expression common enough.

Though the function of words in our lives is to communicate, we do not communicate by words alone. Young babies express emotions and communicate their wants by screams and other non-verbal noises; and so do most of us under the stress of very strong emotion. If I see a girl weeping, wish to say something helpful and cannot think of any useful expression, to place a hand on her shoulder may be enough to communicate what she will feel as a good deal of sympathy. If, on the other hand, someone is angry with me and indicates the door with a dramatic gesture I shall not suppose that he wants me to eat nuts and raisins with him. Often when we are in a foreign country and do not know the language we resort to more elaborate gesture as a means of expressing our feelings, making requests or being polite to people. Pictures may be a form of communication, either as the work of artists who wish to share their vision with others, or as actual picture stories (comic strips where words are absent) and primitive picture-writing. Pictures, however, may be misunderstood; Kipling's story *How the Alphabet was Made* illustrates this possibility brilliantly; and there is the old story of the tourist in Spain who, having sketched an ox and a mushroom to indicate that he would like a steak with mushrooms, was given a sunshade and a ticket for the bullfight. A recent publication for tourists who can neither learn languages nor draw consist entirely of clear pictures of things a tourist may be expected to need; it should be very useful; but it would be difficult to say in pictures 'I will do this if it is legal in your country' or even 'I am allergic to eggs'—which is concrete enough, but not easy to represent pictorially!

Music has sometimes been said to be an international language. It does certainly communicate; in particular, some music communicates moods and emotions; but it does not, on the whole, communicate the same things as words communicate; it is certainly no substitute for words.

One of the differences, so far as we know, between human beings and animals is that while the courtship and mating of animals is entirely material, sensitive human beings often feel a kind of personal communication when they caress each other. A clasp of the hand, a kiss, an embrace, may be much more than a pleasure; it may be an expression of emotion, sometimes at least seeming to be more adequate than verbal expressions. Friends as well as sweethearts often caress one another as an expression of emotion—welcome, sympathy, reconciliation, congratulation, gratitude and so on. Indeed, there have on occasions been tragedies because a communicative caress between friends was misinterpreted as an expression of passion.

However, there is no substitute for words. All other forms of human communication are, by their very nature, confined to certain fields of expression: either, as with pictures, to the simplest concrete ideas, or, as with caresses and inarticulate noises, to the expression of emotion. Only words can communicate nearly the whole range of human experience. (Mystics and those who have experienced very deep love, with a few others, will admit that some of their experiences cannot be described in the language at their disposal.) Thus words are very important if we are not to live in solitude.

Unfortunately we do not naturally know how to use words; even the most intelligent and articulate people quite often have to say, 'I don't quite know how to put this . . .' and human beings often say to each other something like, 'Why can't you say what you mean?' We have to train ourselves to use words properly, not only from the point of view of the grammarian, but from the point of view of meaning. It does not really matter much if we say, for instance, 'Jimmy has eated Peter's cake!' instead of *eaten*; we shall still be understood; but if we say, 'Jimmy is always a wicked boy and a thief!' under the provocation of a single, perhaps not at all typical, act of cake-stealing, we are seriously misusing words and may do Jimmy great harm.

Words, alas, can be misused. They can be used to lie, to evade, and as an excuse for not acting. No more skill in using the vocal organs, no more intelligence, is required to say 'Jimmy has stolen Peter's cake' if this statement is untrue. The idea that it is better to speak the truth than to lie does not seem to be born in us; moreover, very few people live in situations in which it is possible never to tell an untruth. The question of deliberate truth-telling and deliberate lying is a moral question; we can ourselves choose to do one or the other, and the importance we give to the matter, together with the views we hold on truth-telling—for instance, whether we may tell an untruth to protect someone else, or to protect ourselves from obviously bad and vindictive people—involve questions outside the scope of this book.

Words can be used to evade problems and conceal situations. Much propaganda by governments has something of this character. 'The rioting is now at an end' says one government when the market square is strewn with dead workmen. 'Reactionary elements have been eliminated' says another, when its prisons are full of suffering and bewildered people who have done nothing generally recognized as wrong. 'We are looking into your complaint', says the firm, meaning 'We hope you will forget about it if we delay long enough.'

Words can also be used as an excuse for inaction. It is much easier to sympathize profusely with someone than to help, to make some beautiful noises about our country or our cause than to make sacrifices, to reproach ourselves for our faults than to make the effort to overcome them. Once in a Midland chapel some men began to talk about another member of the congregation who was absent that evening. He had been seriously hurt in an accident at work, compensation was being delayed by legal arguments, his wife was ill and the whole family was in great difficulties. Everyone began to express regret: 'How sad that such a fine man should be in such trouble!' 'Makes you wonder why these things have to happen!' 'Such a pity, and they are such a happy couple.' 'I am very sorry for them.' This went on for some minutes until a simple but sincere man, hearing the twentieth 'I feel so sorry for them . . .' suddenly put some notes on the table and said, 'I am sorry five pounds. How much are you sorry?' The result was a large collection that relieved the family's immediate needs. One of the problems of life is to know when to stop talking and begin acting; if we do it too soon, we may make wrong decisions through our haste, and if we leave it too late action may be useless.

Most of us have had the experience of hearing someone stir up a great dust of words so that people cannot think. Politicians frequently do this; so do advertisers; so do most of us in family or personal quarrels.

These uses of words, however, are a matter of wrong conduct not of intellectual mistakes. This book is concerned with saying what we mean when we intend to say it, and understanding what other people mean. The study of the meaning of words is called *semantics* or *semasiology*. The former word is the one more often used for the popular or elementary study of the subject and is the word I shall use hereafter in this book. It might perhaps be said that the aim of popular semantics is to *teach us not to lie except on purpose.* If we want to lie on purpose, we need moral, not semantic, guidance, just as there is a difference between the man who falls over the kerb because he did not see it, and the one who falls where there is no kerb because he has had too much beer.

A great deal of advanced research into semantics is being done at present. Much of this is very specialized and difficult, requires a special vocabulary and is unintelligible except to a reader trained in linguistic studies, or philosophy, or preferably both; but everyone can study elementary semantics with advantage.

Many people will say at this point, 'But it is not hard to know what words mean! We know the meaning of all the ordinary words, and when we hear or see hard unusual words we can look them up in a dictionary!' In fact the question of what words mean is not as simple as it looks.

Suppose we take a very simple word such as *air*. We do not know what this word means until we have a context for it. It means something different in each of these sentences: 'She strolled in the garden humming a cheerful air.' 'This room is stuffy; we need some fresh air.' 'I don't like his arrogant air.' 'Air my shirt and brush my coat, please.' The easiest words to define are the words that look difficult, the technical words, for a technical word generally means only one idea: *vertebrate, anacoluthon, longitude, ampere,* are much more sharply definable than such a word as *door,* or *beautiful,* or even *blue.*

It does not seem likely that even specialists in semantics use words as precision tools all day. When such an expert finds that his car will not start, he is quite capable of saying something like 'This diabolical, infernal tin can is misbehaving again!' though the car is not diabolically possessed, was obtained from a second-hand car dealer and not from hell, is not a tin can, and, having no moral consciousness, cannot misbehave. However, once we become conscious that saying what we mean is quite a difficult matter, we shall at least be more careful in the use of words when they are important— and more suspicious of words when suspicion is no bad thing.

Once I had a class of charming girls whose written work was rather slovenly. Tired of covering their exercises with red streaks, I one day preached them a fierce little sermon on the subject of saying what we mean. 'Don't use words that mean nothing!' I said sternly. 'Don't waffle and pad! Words are supposed to mean something! And be careful how you use words; say what you mean and not something rather like it.' In this vein I continued for some minutes. At the end of my little sermon I said, 'Now, at least for today try to say what you mean and not something vague or inexact.' One girl, who had a sweet and candid nature, but who had probably never before encountered the idea that saying what we mean was an aspect of sincerity and the quest for truth, must have listened with great attention, for later she was asked a question:

'By the way, who wrote *Kubla Khan?*'

'It was Shelley. . . .' She saw the expression on my face.

'I *think* it was Shelley. . . .' I gather that the expression on my face did not improve, for she finally adopted the version: 'At least, er, I *hope* it was Shelley!'

She had grasped the general idea.

II. THE KEY TO UNDERSTANDING

C AN we define *understanding*, from the point of view of the person who hears or reads the words, and *saying what we mean*, from the point of view of the speaker or writer? Obviously these are two sides of the same coin. *Understanding* is itself a rather difficult word to define: for example, a person who has had the experience of love or bereavement will in one sense understand a love poem or an elegy far more than a less experienced person; a historian and a plumber may both perfectly well understand an article about some urns and bones recently dug up in Mesopotamia, but the historian is likely to perceive implications in the facts that the plumber cannot perceive; two people may both understand an order to do a certain piece of work, and carry out the order, but one may do it better than the other, having more knowledge, more skill, or more experience of what will best please the employer. For the moment we are concerned only with the verbal understanding of words: that Mary, told 'Please bring me my hat' shall bring a hat, rather than gloves or a piece of cheese, not that she shall realize that the speaker wants her mauve straw hat, not her brown felt hat.

A working definition that will do for the semantic problems of everyday life is: *understanding is adequate when a word or group of words means the same to speaker and hearer, or writer and reader.*

This may be illustrated by reference to a few material

13

objects first. A man from Staffordshire who said to a Scotsman: 'Roll up your sausage in an oatcake' would seem to be giving ridiculous advice. Staffordshire oatcakes are large, limp and pliable; Scots oatcakes are smaller and more like biscuits. To me the word *starved* means 'in serious need of food'. I am somewhat stout, and was much surprised some years ago when, in another part of England, I called on an old lady on a frosty day and was cordially welcomed with the words: 'Come in, come in, my poor dear, you look quite starved!' In her part of the country *starved* meant *cold*. To some people a *tabby cat* is a cat striped in a characteristic pattern, to others a female cat. Most English people use the term *salame* to refer to any continental sausage of the rich, hard, solid kind that one can hang up in the kitchen and keep for a long time; but when a Pole offered me something of this kind and I said, 'Ah, thank you; I like salame very much . . .' he was quite annoyed, saying, 'This is not salame, this is proper sausage. Salame is made from donkey meat!'

As soon as we move into the realm of more abstract ideas the possibility of misunderstanding increases. What are *young women*? Women under twenty-five? thirty? thirty-five? or even forty? To a child of ten a forty-year-old may seem so old as to be utterly remote, incomprehensible, uncomprehending. Yet a fifty-year-old may make the often disastrous mistake of treating an eighteen-year-old like a child, because to him or her the eighteen-year-old seems so very young.

'The Browns are a wonderfully happy couple.'

'You are quite mistaken; it shows how appearances deceive; I once saw them have a nasty quarrel and shout at each other.'

'I can believe that, but fundamentally they are a very happy couple; they care about one another, their temperaments are suited and they are very loyal to one another.'

The Key to Understanding

'Well, I don't call that happiness; it isn't a bit like what you see on the pictures. It sounds very dull.'

These two people may both be quite sincere; but their definitions of a happy marriage would be considerably different.

Even an apparently simple phrase like *enough to eat* may need to be carefully examined. Such a question may be very important to someone's happiness: 'Are the prisoners getting enough to eat?' 'The children in the orphanage must have enough to eat, but we cannot afford to give them more than enough.' Does *enough to eat* mean enough to keep a person alive, in whatever state of health; enough of a variety of foods to keep a person in good health; enough food to cause an increase in body weight; or as much food as the person wishes to eat? Obviously the interpretation put on the phrase may make an important difference to the diet.

The sentence *I love you* may reasonably lay claim to be the most beautiful sentence in the English language. It is also one of the most tragically ambiguous. Parents say they love their children, and cramp the children's lives, expect disproportionate returns of love and never really relinquish their children to the marriage partner or the vocation. Friends say they love, and monopolize. Almost every adult person has probably some memory of suffering caused because a man and a woman, perhaps both well-meaning, used the words *I love you* in two different senses without realizing it. It is important that we should know what we mean by love in ourselves and what we expect other people to mean; and if there is any doubt whatever, the matter needs to be discussed. For 'I love you' may mean anything from 'I value your personality so much that I would like to do all I could to help it to grow and be happy' to 'I want you all to myself and you must never feel any affection or desire for anyone else', and even to 'I want to kiss you so much that it is cruel of you not to let me.'

The Key to Understanding

The fact that two people can understand the same words in different senses gives rise to a great deal of amusement; it is the cause of many puns and double-meaning jokes. A friend of mine from Yugoslavia, a very good needlewoman, once saw me in a bad state of nervous tension, and said, 'My sewing helps me to be calm: Marjorie, what a peety you are not a sewer!'

I knew a doctor, a man of excellent physique, personal charm and chivalrous manners, who was married very happily and had two children. One day he was asked to visit a sick girl in a farmhouse. It was harvest-time and every well person was out of doors; so no one let him in and he walked slowly upstairs to look for the girl's bedroom. As his steps sounded on the stair, the girl began to scream. 'It's all right, it's all right!' he reassured her, but the screams grew more piercing as he approached. As his head appeared round the bedroom door the sick girl suddenly became calm and exclaimed, 'Oh, Doctor, I'm so glad it's you! I thought it was a man!'

I was once at a conference where a number of ladies, all most respectable, sat at a long table for lunch. One of us was asked to serve the food. For each course there was a choice of two dishes. We all tried to help by passing our requests to the server. One lady caused some amusement by saying cheerfully, 'I'm a rissole!' but when the sweet course arrived there was quite a scandal. Someone who had been helpfully enquiring what her neighbours preferred said in a fine loud conference voice, 'We're all tarts at this end of the table!'

'I can't stop for pudding,' said a busy woman at another lunch. 'I'm all behind already.' The unfortunate thing was that the lower part of her torso was indeed rather disproportionately large.

I was lecturing and noticed that a student fidgeted constantly. I raised my eyebrows at her once or twice; no result. I tried to make my lecture more interesting; she still wriggled and shifted. Eventually I could stand this no longer and asked her: 'Are you unwell, or what is it?' 'No, thank you; I'm sorry to keep moving, but I think I must have a screw loose!' She undoubtedly meant, in the tubular chair on which she was sitting, but her classmates did not take it that way.

Recently I greatly enjoyed an Esperanto lecture tour in Sweden, where I met with magnificent hospitality and was entertained by a number of very charming, kindly and interesting people. I think I must have talked a little too much about my trip, for on one occasion a colleague at the lunch table passed me the vegetable dish with a very pointed, 'You like swedes very much, don't you?' I fell into the trap, too, with a sincere and innocent, 'Oh, yes!'

Such ambiguities have their uses. They amuse people and spice our lives. The really dangerous ambiguities are not those which we all notice and which make us laugh, but those which we do not notice at all.

'Enough to eat' . . . 'I love you' . . . 'Civilized behaviour' . . . 'my Christian duty' . . . what do we mean by these expressions? It may be very important. 'The prisoners all have enough to eat' we are told, and are satisfied that they are treated with humanity in the matter of food. In fact no one has died of starvation: the prisoners are merely so weak that they cannot work and ridden with scurvy. 'I love you!' says a boy to a girl, and she thinks that when they are married life will be as easy as eating strawberries, a continual ecstasy. Poor girl . . . yet her boy may mean something quite sincere and quite worth having. 'Civilized behaviour' to some people means going to theatres and listening to long-playing records, knowing which fork to use and not wearing curlers in the street; to others it may imply trying not to be jealous, tolerating the opinions of others, and setting differences by argument and compromise rather than a punch on the nose. A woman once declared that she burned her small child with a hot poker for stealing a few biscuits because it was her 'Christian duty'!

I suppose there has never been a political speech or an election address that did not contain examples of language whose meaning was doubtful—even when the words were used in good faith. Two people who officially belong to the same religious group may be found, if their ideas are carefully investigated, to have very widely different concepts about the things they say they believe. A person who says, 'I believe in discipline!' may be anything from a cruel martinet, always punishing, rebuking and regimentating, to someone who merely has a preference for habits of hard work, punctuality and self-control. What does the word 'democracy' mean? To some it refers mostly to constitutional qualities and is almost a synonym for parliamentary government with some safeguards for civil liberties; to others it is mostly a matter of the absence of class distinctions; and to some people in eastern Europe it appears to refer to economic rather than political organization and to be used in quite a different sense from that understood in America.

Let us take two simple words, each of one syllable, each used by everyone at least once a day. What do we mean when we say 'a good man' and 'a bad man'? I am fairly certain that a discussion group of ten people, especially (but not necessarily) if they were drawn from different religious groups and social classes, and were of assorted ages and both sexes, would produce ten different definitions. This is partly because we all tend to value most those virtues that come most easily to us, and to condone most readily those faults that we find it hardest to overcome; partly because we have been brought up with different assumptions about goodness and badness. For example, I have actually heard it said more than once, 'I have been lucky: I had very good parents, very strict.' To me this is a contradiction in terms: I, though I do not believe in anarchy in the home, could never be convinced that a strict parent can possibly be a truly good parent, or that someone with strict parents can possibly be thought of as lucky; and I could defend my views in much detail. I was once paid a magnificent backhanded compliment when a young girl, of what most people would call very decent character, came, in great anxiety, to consult me about one of those trivial sexual problems that can reduce an adolescent to obsessive misery and can be set right in five minutes with a little rudimentary biological information. I gave the girl the information she needed, reassured her and made her happy again, then said, 'Now, if ever you are worried about anything like that, remember I am here; don't make yourself miserable, but come and see me and I will try to help you.' I then added, not wishing to usurp the functions of a parent, 'But of course the best person to confide in over things like that is your mother.' 'Oh,' cried my young friend, with intense feeling, 'I couldn't possibly talk to my mother about a thing like that! You see, my mother is a good woman!'

'Thanks very much!' I said, laughing; but the remark threw a lurid light on some people's notion of goodness.

Most human beings would, if asked, say that *justice* or *fairness* was something good, desirable. But justice is not as easy to define as we may at first think. Suppose, for example, two men each commit the crime of stealing the same sum of money, each from an infirm old woman who kept the same type of shop, and each at dusk. If these cases were reported with only those details in the newspaper, on the same day, and one man had been sentenced to two years' imprisonment while the other received a conditional discharge, most people would be shocked at the 'injustice'. Yet suppose one thief had been a strong, healthy man of thirty, capable of work, in an area where there was little unemployment, a man with a comfortable home, who was known to the old woman and had received various kindnesses from her; and the other thief had been a man whose mind had been disturbed by horrible war experiences, whose wife was in hospital recovering from a dangerous operation and who desperately wanted more money to buy delicacies for her? He would still be doing wrong, but most of us would agree that his crime was not as deserving of severe punishment.

I do not care to commit myself to opinions on every detail of politics: I know just enough about politics, from a reading of numerous books and two responsible papers, to be aware that I do not know very much. (This is unfortunately a rare and very valuable piece of knowledge.) In general, however, I know that I stand somewhere to left of centre, that I am strongly opposed to all forms of totalitarianism, that I think force in politics should be avoided as much as possible, and that political behaviour should be governed mostly by what many would call humanitarian considerations; to me the business of government should be to promote the happiness of the people governed and, as far as possible, of the rest of the world. I am also very much aware that considerations of immediate expediency do often have to take precedence over ideals for the time being, and that the most desirable reforms can often not be made in a hurry. With this kind of moderate and tolerant left-wing-liberal-humanitarian-rationalist political background, I have in the course of time been called: A Fascist sympathizer, a Bolshevik, a traitor to my country, hopelessly naïve, far too subtle, a dreamy idealist and a terrible cynic; I have also been bitterly and torrentially scolded for not caring enough about the agony of World War Two, and lectured at considerable length about the stupidity of caring as much as I do about the sufferings of the World War Two victims. I hope I deserved none of these things; but I certainly cannot deserve all of them. Name-calling in politics is very largely the result of slack definitions, and will be discussed more fully in the next chapter. If political name-calling remained an affair of words, it would not much matter except as a breach of courtesy; but name-calling not infrequently leads to blood-shedding or at least to victimization; so it does matter very much.

III. SOME CAUSES OF MISUNDERSTANDING

MISUNDERSTANDING of words can arise in many ways other than lying on the part of the speaker or downright stupidity on the part of the hearer. Some common misunderstandings may be classified under headings.

I. MALAPROPISM

In either (a) the speaker or (b) the hearer. The word is well known to be derived from the popular character Mrs. Malaprop (*Mal à propos*—inappropriate) in Sheridan's comedy *The Rivals*. Mrs. Malaprop wants to appear well-educated and uses long words without knowing their meaning, saying *epitaphs* for *epithets*, *odorous* for *odious* and so on. I have been informed that the housewife using an electric stove should make full use of the *residential* heat (*residual*); and that diet should be suited to the *digestibility* of the family! The schoolboy with a passion for aeroplanes thought an *aviary* was a place in which research of aviation was carried out; and a timid girl said she did not like parties because she was not really *socialist* (*sociable*). I heard of a woman who was disproportionately offended when a welfare worker advised special teaching for her *illiterate* young son, and angrily produced her marriage lines. (*Illegitimate* being the word she thought she heard.) I was much puzzled when in the school laboratory I first saw a *desiccator*—a lidded jar containing a water-attracting substance and used for drying things—for I knew only the *desiccated coconut* in the larder at home and could not see how a jar could possibly cut any substance up into tiny pieces.

There was the engaging little girl who, told that twins were two babies born at the same time, said, 'Please, miss, I know what it is when there are three—*giblets*!' There may also be the malapropism of pronunciation: I was once told 'Don't step on that poodle!' by an Oriental, who was in fact warning me not to step in a large puddle. I was once asked by a Japanese girl if I could possibly send her a 'small *rocket*'. It took some time to realize that what she wanted was a small *locket*. If a keeper in a zoo warned me 'There's a *moose* got out!' it would be useful to know if he were English or Scottish! There was recently an argument in the Press as to the precise degree of poverty suffered in an Eastern country. Some said the country people were reduced to eating *mice*; but others said that this was a mishearing or mispronunciation over the telephone of *maize*.

Most misunderstandings that arise from malapropism can be cleared up by someone who sees what has happened, or by reference to a dictionary. It is, however, wise to remember that a dictionary can be very misleading. A *tetrameter* does indeed 'have four feet', but a rabbit is not a tetrameter. *Claustrophobia*, 'fear of being confined' must not be further interpreted as reluctance to have children.

Misunderstandings caused by malapropisms are generally amusing, at least afterwards, and relatively seldom do harm. More serious are the misunderstandings that may arise out of

2. DIFFERENCES OF DEFINITION

These may arise even in the ordinary details of practical life, as with *oatcake* or *salcme* quoted in the previous chapter. What is a *house*? This question may be important with regard to rates, taxes and other legal obligations. There is a story told of a biologist who took a large number of specimens on a train many years ago. He asked the booking clerk what tickets he would have to buy for his various animals. The booking clerk was not sure and sought the help of the station-master. Together they thumbed through the regulations and finally came to the following startling conclusion: 'Well, seems as if dogs is dogs, and bear cubs is dogs, and anteaters is dogs, and wild cats is dogs, and kestrels is dogs, but tortoises is insects, and goes free!' There was a considerable difference here between zoological and railway-regulation definition. What is a *vehicle*? For example, if someone lives in an old bus, is it a house or a vehicle with regard to legal obligations?

In wartime, in all communities, conduct likely to lower the public will to victory is normally forbidden and punished. Here again questions of definition are important. Perhaps the only punishable offence is to state publicly that the enemy has right on his side, to insist that one's own country cannot possibly win or to urge people to revolt against the government. In some countries, however, where such regulations against 'sedition' or 'hindering the war effort' have been in in force, people have been severely punished for grumbling about a shortage of potatoes.

What is *sabotage*? In England the term is normally confined to the deliberate hindering of some state or occasionally private activity by damaging machinery, holding up supplies or giving dangerously false information. In a number of countries accidental hindering of state work is punished as sabotage; and indeed the term—implying heavy penalties— may even apply to the supporting of opinions or policies which subsequently did not succeed or which went out of favour with the government. What, again, is a *traitor*? To most people, if they stop to think, a traitor is someone who intentionally injures his country or his cause, and this very strong word carries the implication both of important harmful action and of malice. It is, however, not unusual for someone to receive abusive letters calling him a traitor because he is a conscientious objector to military service—a man in a very special and difficult moral position, which usually means he has high principles, however much others may disagree with him—because he has publicly criticized something wrong in the life of the country or because he has foreign friends.

Many people think they agree about religion until they begin to discuss it. What are the real meanings of such words as *sin*, *salvation*, *God*, the *Holy Spirit*, the *pure in heart*, the *Church*, the *Will of God*, or even *Christianity*? Most of us have read of violent argument as to the implications of 'Christian marriage' and 'Church unity', for example. A very naïve person and an archbishop may both believe that 'When I die, I may go to Heaven' but their interpretations of Heaven may be unrecognizable as the same concept. Some people say that the only real *sin* is hurting other people on purpose or by negligence; others say that *sin* is setting our own wishes before the will of God; and a clergyman once told me: 'The trouble with most of my flock is that they think *sin* is something-pleasant-you-can-do-with-your-body, and that if they have no fun they are sure to be righteous!'

People have, in the past, tortured and burned one another over questions of the definition of the terms of religion. Nowadays religious persecution occurs in only a few countries, and seldom extends to murder; but people who are concerned with religion are still apt to misunderstand one another because they have not thought what their words really mean. Such misunderstandings may be very important for mental health, for personal happiness, for good conduct, and, a good many would say, for our hope of salvation. Surely the woman who thought 'Christian duty' could dictate that she burn a child with hot iron was trapped in an appalling misunderstanding that did matter, that was much more than just a small point about words? Surely the mistake of those who think 'purity' is attainable only by those who, having defective glands, never have any thought of sex, is a mistake that is no dictionary quibble, but can matter very much indeed? The most wretched, tortured neurotic I ever met had learned in childhood that 'God' meant a kind of gigantic headmaster, vindictive and alert, who was perpetually watching her to see if she 'sinned' and to punish her, far more unreasonably than any human authority, for the most trivial mistake in life. What people mean when they use the word 'God' may colour their whole mode of life: may make a person radiantly patient, unselfish, merciful and helpful, or may create an obsessed inquisitor and persecuting monster. So definitions do matter very much indeed.

In the field of general morality, too, very serious misunderstandings may arise from differences of definition. Anna, we are told, is a *bad girl*. On investigation, this may prove to mean that she wears rather a lot of costume jewellery, sometimes stays out at night after ten and likes the company of boys. A religious worker once reported to me that she had heard a woman say of her own child, in public, 'She is a very naughty little girl; she is afraid of pussy-cats!' What is *honesty*? Not to steal and not to cheat the income-tax? Most of us would agree that these are a part of honesty; but some would add that it involves not pretending to be something we are not; and some, that it includes doing our paid work as well as we can. Large numbers of people seem genuinely to believe that it is not *dishonest* to cheat the State or to steal or damage Government property, which comes, for them, in a special category. Yet if we reflect that Government property and income come out of our taxes, the person who robs the Government is indirectly robbing his neighbours, not to mention himself.

Some Causes of Misunderstanding

A man had for years accepted numerous favours from others without any attempt at making any return when he could; he had shamefully exploited his housekeeper; and he had eventually cheated a relative of his inheritance. Near to death, he said, 'I am not afraid; I have never done anyone any harm.' He was probably quite sincere; *harm* meant to him giving someone a black eye or throwing him downstairs!

What is *patriotism*? To some it means sacrificing various aspects of personal convenience to the country. To others it means mostly taking a pride in the culture and valuable achievements of the country, perhaps being proud of such things (in England) as that the country generally takes its treaty obligations seriously, or that it accepts refugees and usually treats them well. To others *patriotism* means defending their country when its policies are morally questionable, and noisily expressing hatred for all other nations. An amusing aspect of this is that, as strongly nationalistic governments are those most likely to cause political upheavals, very 'patriotic' people of the latter variety usually show most disapproval for those political leaders who, in their own countries, are themselves the most 'patriotic'.

'I think we have a few things to be proud of,' I was saying to the foreign visitors. 'We really do in England have more freedom than in most of the world. I would like to show you one of our good new schools—I think if I telephone the headmaster he will make arrangements for us. You may smile at our kindness to animals, but I think it is rather a nice tradition and helps to train us in gentleness. You won't often see ragged people in England today. Of course, I know our cooking is a joke; it is better, generally, in homes than in restaurants, but I must admit we cannot generally cook as well as you do. Please don't look afraid of that policeman; our policemen are always polite and helpful to strangers.'

Someone took me aside and hissed furiously in my ear: 'I think you ought to be ashamed of yourself, running your country down in front of those damned foreigners!'

It took me some time to realize it must be the bit about the cooking that he meant.

I was once rather sorry to hear that a girl I liked was *promiscuous*. This properly means much the same as *indiscriminate*, and is nowadays applied mostly to people's sexual behaviour. In this sphere real *promiscuity* (having any number of lovers with no sort of genuine choice or affection) is relatively very rare. I thought the girl could hardly be as promiscuous as that, but wondered if she were in fact somewhat lacking in restraint and discrimination. Eventually I found out that my informant meant merely that the girl was in the habit, when opportunity offered, of kissing her fiancé and had sometimes been seen doing this! So far from being *promiscuous*, she was, by all usual standards, the opposite— *faithful*! But some people use the word *promiscuous* to refer to any sexual behaviour of which they personally do not approve. My informant could probably have been sued for slander.

Misunderstandings may arise, not from actual differences of definition, but more from what might be called

3. DIFFERENCES OF ASSOCIATION

An aunt and I were walking in a rather poor district in an industrial town. My aunt noticed that a boy of perhaps seven or eight had a wound over one eye. She slightly knew him, and asked sympathetically, 'How did you get your eye hurt?' The child replied, as though it was the most usual thing in the world, 'Daddy done it.'

To seven-year-old Paul, his daddy is a wonderful person, who gives him treats, tells him stories, takes him for rides on his back, and is fair to him. Sometimes daddy is cross; but he does listen to what Paul has to say for himself, and Paul adores him.

At school these two little boys are told that 'God is like a father to all of us.'

The inferences from their experience of fathers will lead them to very different ideas about God!

Associations attached to words may differ for several reasons, some of which—not an exhaustive list—being:

(a) *Social Position.* Among poor people 'He has a car' will be said with some tone of admiration, envy, or possibly disapproval of such excessive wealth. Among people whose general income level is such that a car is taken more or less for granted, the statement has no emotional colouring; it is just a statement of fact, probably a confirmation of what was supposed. I can imagine that there may be people, though I have never known any, among whom 'He has a car' implies that he is a poor fellow who cannot afford a helicopter or a yacht.

A word such as *gentleman* or *lady* may mean very different things for people in different social groups. For example, I heard a rather poor girl, who had had a hard life, say that in the sanatorium where she was being treated she could not *lead a lady's life.* This to her meant that she was expected to do some work. To another person a *lady* is someone who, among other things, has a spirit of service and helpfulness and often works very hard. Among some groups *to be talked about* implies something regarded as desirable; to others it is something to be avoided at all costs.

Some people who work with their hands genuinely do not believe that lawyers, teachers, or Civil Servants *work*; their concept of work does not include mental effort; it is even commoner to suppose that writers and artists do not *work*, though in fact their work requires great concentration as well as skill, much effort as well as knowledge. Conversely, many professional people do not regard farming, mining, deep-sea fishing or making pottery as demanding *intelligence*, and may presume to despise those who do such work, forgetting that these tasks require skill, knowledge, concentration and intelligence as well as physical effort. Ideas of what constitutes a *hard* or an *easy* life will vary considerably according to the social group. Occasionally the interpretation will not be what one might pardonably expect; for example, in some rich homes where the sons are sent to public schools the parents accept without distress that the boys may be severely corporally punished, whereas many a mother has come out of a factory to make fierce complaints against the teacher who has been 'knocking my lad about'. In this respect at least to be born with a silver spoon in the mouth would seem to be a disadvantage. To some people a bathroom is more of a *necessity* than a television set; to quite a number of people today the reverse seems to be true. *Rich* and *poor* are other words that will very obviously depend for their meaning on the social group to which speaker or hearer belongs.

(b) *Generation*. Some words do actually change with the passage of time; more will be said about this in Chapter VI. The associations of a word, however, also change with the passage of time, and a person of one generation may have quite different clusters of association round a word from those of another. For example, the word *actress* has greatly gained in respectability in several generations. The word *Empire*, on the other hand, once a word always to be spoken with pride and enthusiasm, is now an uncomfortable word for many, savouring too much of jingoism and power-hunger. The word *divorce* was once a good deal more startling than it is now; and with the shedding of taboos a good many words (most of them perfectly neutral anatomical and medical terms) are spoken naturally by the younger generation, whereas some people still surviving can pronounce them only in a whisper or with visible difficulty.

School will carry very different associations for one who was beaten, bored and humiliated there and for one who was well treated, had interesting lessons and was able to respect his or her teachers. *Housewife* and *housework* arouse very different feelings in the minds of two women, one of whom has had to drudge all her life in an ill-planned home and for an unappreciative family, and one of whom has a modern convenient home, a good knowledge of how to do her work happily and a family that gives her love and thanks. Another interesting difference between the generations results from progress in medical science. For instance, only one or two generations ago the word *pneumonia* carried with it a frightened hush, because pneumonia was very commonly fatal. With the general use of new drugs, it has ceased to be a death warrant and is spoken of in a more casual tone.

As the world grows smaller such words as *foreigner* and *coloured man* lose associations of hostility and terror that they once had. Where a sixty-year-old may still finish her cautionary tale with the words 'and she married a black man!', the thirty-year-old is quite likely to reply—though preferably in more polite diction—'So what?'

Disputes between the generations sometimes include semantic difficulties which would be amusing if only they were not so uncomfortable for all concerned. We have all heard this kind of thing:

'You know I am not an unreasonable mother; all I ask is that you behave sensibly. But when it comes to staying out till a quite unreasonable hour. . . .'

'But, Mother, half-past ten is not an unreasonable hour! The pictures don't finish till quarter-past. It isn't reasonable to expect me to leave until they are over!'

'And this doing yourself up with lipstick and all manner

of paint, looking like a trollop! I've tried to bring you up respectable, and look at you!'

'Oh, do be reasonable! All smart girls wear lipstick nowadays!'

'Not a bit of a kid like you!'

'I'm not a bit of a kid at sixteen, and I'm not going to go about like a dowdy old frump!'

And so it goes on, with no one trying to think what *reasonable* means, both sides exaggerating, as useless and exhausting as a conversation between diplomatists both of whom are instructed to make no compromises. . . .

The associations often differ for different generations because the invention or other object or experience has become more widely available. To my own mother in youth *a banana* was a luxury fruit, rather what *lichees* are to me; nowadays a banana normally carries practically no luxury or rarity associations. During World War Two, incidentally, the word *egg* acquired exciting associations that it had not had for a very long time. Shell eggs were rare; hence the shift of association. In my own childhood *television* was something one read about in science fiction. Very possibly to a child born two or three generations after me *artificial satellite* will carry no associations of wonder and hardly arouse interest.

(c) *Sex*. A man and a woman will sometimes hear a word with different reactions because their associations are different. The most obvious example of this is the words *man* and *woman*, together with *boy* and *girl*, *husband* and *wife*, *father* and *mother*. For the opposite sex is always more or less mysterious: the experience of the other sex, not only in family life but in the whole life-process from beginning to end, is something into which we can, it seems, never enter fully; and words denoting the opposite sex will also tend to be loaded with associations of either resentment or interest, depending on various factors of society, upbringing and experience.

Home generally seems to carry more rich and interesting associations for a woman; *war* and *revolution* generally seem to carry a few romantic and colourful associations for a man whereas for a woman they almost always imply mere dread and tragedy; this seems odd, in that men still do most of the actual fighting in most wars; perhaps the natural biological interests of the two sexes account for the difference. The sex association-patterns of words also changes as the exact limits of the functions of men and women change; for instance, now that there have been a few women professors, the word *professor* will have, for both sexes, slightly different sets of associations; in societies where a married woman is a household drudge and has very few civil rights, it may be expected that the word *mistress* will carry much more glamour, and even a kind of dignity, than in a society in which married women are allowed a good deal of freedom and initiative.

A woman hearing the word *hat*, with nothing to qualify it, will probably visualize a woman's hat and a man will visualize a man's hat; similarly with other garments. A man hearing the word *knife* is much more likely to think of a pocket-knife than a woman, who will probably think first of a table or kitchen knife. The word *powder* by itself once meant gunpowder to the colonel and hair or face powder to his lady. And so on.

(d) *Occupation.* The likelihood of actual misunderstanding arising out of the fact that the same word carries a different set of associations for a person in another occupation is very limited; but the differences of association are real enough. For example:

Watch has different first meanings for a watchmaker and a sailor.

Chestnut—for a greengrocer, a comedian and a horse-breeder.

Slug—for a gunsmith and a gardener.

Cat—for a veterinary surgeon and a prison governor.

Case—for a porter and a printer.

Scissors—for a wrestler and a seamstress.

Plug—for a plumber, a tobacconist, and an electrician.

Form—for a school-teacher and a Civil Servant.

Seat—for a carpenter and a Member of Parliament.

Sole—for the shoemaker and the fishmonger. And when a girl on a rather strenuous country walk exclaimed, 'I can't walk fast; I am losing my sole!' her companions wondered if a clergyman might not be needed too.

Ham—for an actor and the owner of a delicatessen shop.

Again, a word like *harvest* or *warble fly* is far richer in associations to a farmer than to a typist; and it is a standing joke that what to a landsman is a *gale* is to an experienced sailor a *gentle breeze*.

(e) *General Personal Experience.* It is not at all uncommon to find that people have a few words or names they do not like, not because they dislike what the words or names are supposed to 'mean', but because for them personally some disagreeable associations are attached. Many jokes are based on this fact; for instance, 'I wouldn't ask for a *cheque* today; the boss has just had a row with our representative in Prague, and he is feeling sore on the subject.'

Not only the experience of an individual, but those of the group in which he or she lives, or has been brought up, will give associative colouring to words. For instance, a child can fairly easily be brought up to regard *capitalist* as an insulting or admiring word, to think that *clever* people are people who cheat and avoid work, to associate extreme dislike with a word such as *Jew, nigger, German, Russian,* or *British*; on the whole education can probably give taboos rather sooner than it can remove them and inculcate prejudices rather more easily than tolerance or curiosity.

4. MISUNDERSTANDING OF THE CONTEXT

Very often, when someone asks the meaning of a word, the person asked has to put it in a context, in order to show the meaning, or must even ask the enquirer to provide the context so as to know which of several meanings is required.

'I must have got my threads crossed.'

Is the person handling a screw of some kind, sewing or weaving? Or even in a muddle in a lecture?

The prevailing human tendency to call things by borrowed names, especially in everyday speech, may complicate matters further; *soup* can mean nitro-glycerine, *crate* can mean an aeroplane, *mouse* a variety of surgical swab, and to give somebody *socks* or *beans* may not mean to clothe or feed them.

'I felt wretched, so I went to bed with a bottle.'

Of hot water, or of whisky?

Is *an internal examination* by a doctor or in a college?

If a professional psychologist says someone is an *idiot* in a report, the word is very clearly defined. If he calls someone an idiot in the course of a violent quarrel, *idiot* may merely be an abbreviation for *someone-who-disagrees-with-me*. A lawyer who says 'I'm worried about my new *case*' may be speaking of his profession or of his luggage; until we have a little more context we cannot know.

The possibilities of misunderstanding arising out of various differences in the use of language are, then, enormous. Important differences are more likely to occur in some fields than in others.

IV. VAGUE WORDS AND
EXACT WORDS

IN general, the more language deals with concrete objects the more exact it is; and the most exact language is that of those sciences that deal with the concrete. There is no doubt whatever about the semantics of: *one molecule of copper sulphate; the positive pole of a dry battery; the human vermiform appendix; a 1-dioptre camera lens.* Such expressions have only one meaning.

Moreover, scientists in principle aim at being objective; this discourages the formation of confusing clusters of associations round their words. The only scientific words that inevitably become heavily laden with emotional associations are words that stand for things or phenomena which may affect human life and happiness; there is more emotion attached to, say, *uranium* or *penicillin* than to *helium* or *ferrous oxide*. The scientist is, however, always trying, consciously, to make his language as unambiguous, as objective, as precise as possible. He quite often uses mathematical symbols and formulae, which are even more foolproof than scientific words —provided that one can understand them.

I have no real scientific training; but even the little 'science' one studies at school helps to give some awareness of language as an exact tool; the making and studying of definitions, the following of arguments in mathematics, physics and other sciences, has its uses for showing that some at least of our thinking can be exact.

Vague Words and Exact Words

Ordinary concrete phenomena give rise to language which is not quite as unambiguous as that of science, but which seldom gives rise to serious semantic confusion. A *pie* may be a meat pie or an apple pie, a veal and ham pie or an egg and bacon pie; it may also be a mess of type upset in a printing works; the ordinary man here is at a disadvantage as compared with the mathematician, who has only one *pi* to deal with and multiplies it by the square of the radius to give the area of a circle. . . . But there is a narrow limit to the number of meanings possible for the word *pie*. There are many breeds of dogs, but a point will always come at which the animal being examined is not a *dog*, and everyone has more or less the same idea of the characteristics of a *dog*. A *chair* may be made of upholstered wood and springs, of steel tubes and canvas, of solid wood, of wood and canvas, for that matter of gold, in which case it is more likely to be called a *throne*, but need not be; but, again, we all have some limits in our mind beyond which an object ceases to be a chair. Similarly we have limitations in our minds defining roughly at least such things as *pencil, carpet, rose, toe, frog, button, larder, basket, attic, oar, trough, postcard* and so on. Those limits will not always be precise enough for human requirements; for instance, in assessing objects for Customs duty or purchase tax such questions as 'is this a postcard or a greeting card?' 'Are these buttons or jewellery?' may be quite important and require much discussion. However, in general it is not the names of concrete objects or phenomena that give rise to the most troublesome semantic problems.

Moreover, we know when we do not know the meaning of a word of this kind. If we see a less common name for a concrete object, such as *lemur, conch, orlon, pinking shears, ocarina, alb, malachite,* we know immediately whether we understand the term; and if we do not understand it there is usually very little difficulty in finding out what it means.

Vague Words and Exact Words

We are hardly in danger of basing a wrong action, a catastrophic decision, our own anxiety or misery, on a misconception about the meaning of some word of this kind. And such words generally mean much the same to all the persons who hear or see them. Not quite the same, perhaps; for the surrounding associations may be rich, sparse or even non-existent; but no normal person hearing the word *pie* is in any danger of thinking it means what other people mean when they say *boiled egg*.

I have already given some evidence that even these words do not mean quite the same to everyone, as in the statement 'He has a *car*' or the reactions of two generations to the word *banana*. The semantic advantage of concrete terms is that the limits are much narrower. When we step into the field of abstract language we find ourselves in territory with frighteningly vague frontiers; and, if I may continue my metaphor, the territory is heavily mined; there is real danger in the misunderstanding of many abstract words.

The language of politics is often very ambiguous. Some time ago a cartoon was published showing the representatives of two governments shouting at each other, 'Aggressor!' The *aggressor*, in diplomacy, is supposed to be the government that starts a war or attacks another country. Today almost all governments pay at least lip-service to the idea that *aggression* is wrong and that an aggressor nation should be restrained and punished by others, if possible. This is a step forward from the open power-worship and threatenings of Hitler, but trouble arises as soon as any nation is accused of aggression. Why? Because it is not at all easy, normally, to decide who is really responsible for starting a war. Sometimes it is obvious. If Utopian troops march straight into Ruritania, kill unarmed Ruritanians, loot, burn and wreck, when yesterday relations between the two countries seemed normally quiet, that is clearly aggression; but if large Ruritanian forces had been massing on the frontier for the past fortnight, if unconventionally large numbers of Ruritanian secret agents have been found in Utopia and if the Ruritanian press and radio have for months been pouring out abuse of the Utopian government and urging Utopians to rise against it, the question of who really started the trouble may not be so simple. Today much propaganda work is devoted to proving, where there is tension or actual armed conflict, that the other party was the aggressor—or is expected to be at any moment.

'*Fair shares for all*' is an ideal with which I find myself very much in sympathy; but what exactly does it mean? An assembly could easily agree that they all wanted fair shares for all; then, when the problems of putting this into practice were being discussed, would find that the members could not agree on the details. For example, is it *fair* that all human beings who work should be paid alike? or that they should be paid more if they are showing special skill or taking more responsibility or working in a dangerous or notably unattractive job? Should a married man be paid more than a single man, a man with children than a childless man? Should those who are unlucky enough to be infirm or too mentally deficient to work receive the same share of the community income, or less? Should there be rewards for special efforts? These are by no means easy questions. Even when the principle of *fair shares* is applied to the relatively simple problem of food rationing in wartime, not all the answers are easy. If everyone has exactly the same ration allowance in a time of shortage, children and adolescents will not have enough and their health may be permanently damaged; and if heavy manual workers such as coal miners have to live on the same rations as desk workers, they are not likely to receive enough calories to provide the energy they need. A responsible government has to work out the fairest solutions to such problems that it can devise.

Vague Words and Exact Words

The word *freedom* is another word that causes semantic difficulties. I passionately value freedom; so do most English people; and so, I think, do at least all human beings who have tasted it. But freedom is not ever, and cannot be, absolute. I have no wish to be free to hit my annoying neighbour on the nose; and still less do I wish my neighbour to be free to hit me on the nose. Censorship in some form is probably excessive in nearly every country in the world, by the criteria I accept; but though I believe in 'freedom of speech', I would not like to see freedom even of speech made total, permitting people, without penalty, to say false and ugly things about one another. *The love of freedom* as an emotive phrase is most successful; but as a guide to political action and organization it needs a great deal of careful definition.

All peoples and groups who feel oppressed wish for *liberation*. I remember having as a guest in my home a woman who had spent her most impressionable years in one of the most unfortunate countries in Europe, a country ravaged again and again by war, dictatorship and civil war. One evening I came home from work and set about preparing some supper. 'There's a cake in the tin . . .' I muttered, opened the tin and found no cake. I looked suspiciously at my guest. With a charming smile she explained, 'I've liberated it!' A grim joke, though she did not treat it grimly.

As slogans play a great part in the political thought of many people, it is desirable that we should learn to look at them hard and ask very insistently what they mean.

Many everyday abstract words are equally vague in definition: *good*, *bad*, *sensible*, *strict*, *cheeky*, *greedy*. Here are two reports on the same schoolgirl, from the same report form:

'Joan has a mind of her own and an enquiring attitude. She shows some originality and thinks for herself. She may develop valuable qualities of leadership.'

'Joan has been very cheeky this term and questions the

decisions of those in authority; she is argumentative and apt to be perverse. She is beginning to have a bad influence on her classmates.'

Now some of the difference between these two reports will reflect a real difference in the temperaments and beliefs of two teachers and quite possibly in the objective facts about Joan's behaviour with them; but some of the difference is that their definitions of the key words are different in detail.

The statement that Harold is a *good husband*, that Jill is a *good wife*, that Ethel is a *good mother* or James a *good father*, does not have the same meaning for different people. Even the statement that Helen *eats very little* is not as precise as it sounds; with whose appetite is hers being compared? That Philip *has a hot temper* will probably be taken to mean that he frequently displays violent anger; but the statement does not indicate how often he loses his temper or how quickly he recovers it. One may have a very hot temper—I have myself—and keep it very much under control after years of struggle to do so—I now really lose mine about once a year, but it is still there. Marian *is a flirt*: this may, for different people, mean anything ranging from a total indifference to sex conventions and the feelings of others, to a mere liking for light badinage with men and rather a bright, wandering eye. A housewife boasted that she was *a good cook*. Investigation discovered that she could cook a very limited range of recipes and that, though admittedly she hardly ever spoiled a meal—which for her made her a good cook—none of the meals she cooked were original or exciting and nearly all came out of the frying-pan or a tin.

We cannot get along without these vague abstract words. Moreover, we need not be endlessly examining them all day; life does not afford the time for so much reflection. When Molly tells her mother, 'I have *a very good husband* in John . . .', mother knows all that she really needs or wants to know, which is that her daughter is content with John and will be comparatively happy. The details of Molly's expectations and definitions do not much matter. If I say 'I have *enough* money for my needs' the only thing that matters is that I find it *enough* for me; my own subjective definition will do and my friends or relatives need not be concerned about me. If a doctor says his patient is *getting better now*, the family may want to know whether this still means another month in bed or two days more, but the statement is not in itself without very important meaning. Too much examining of the meaning of words may be downright rude on occasion; some generalizations, some vagueness, are the small change of conversation.

Sometimes, however, the meaning of these words is very important and open to much discussion. In arguments where much emotion is involved, for example, the meaning of a word like *love* or *reasonable* or *selfish* or *fair* is very likely to be used in different senses by different people. More will be said about this in Chapter XII.

Very often the general, abstract words of everyday speech need to be helped out by concrete words that give examples. Concrete advice is generally very plain and not open to misinterpretation:

'You should take two 50 mg. tablets of vitamin C daily and walk in the open air for at least half an hour.' 'To peel tomatoes easily, put them in a basin first and pour some boiling water over them; then the peel will come off loosely.' 'Put an ink-pot at each candidate's place, with one piece of clean blotting-paper and a sharpened pencil.'

This is the kind of language that any intelligent person may be expected to understand. Yet even the most concrete language is sometimes misinterpreted where associations differ; I remember a tale of an elderly countryman with a sore throat. 'Ah,' said the doctor, 'I will give you a throat wash for that.' So the old man was supplied with a large bottle of a mixture labelled: 'Throat wash; to be used when required' —and, instead of gargling with it, ordered his daughter to warm some of the mixture, put it in a basin and carefully wash the outside of his throat with it.

If we are giving advice on general behaviour we shall often find it necessary to illustrate the abstract by means of the concrete.

'You are making a bad impression; you really must try to be more polite to people.'

This is not in itself much use; a person whose manners are bad often just does not think about manners and has no criteria.

'Well, what ought I to do? I didn't think I was being rude.'

'You could hold doors open for people when they are behind you, instead of letting the door bang in their faces; and you could pass the salt and the bread at lunch, instead of leaving all the passing to other people. Oh, and when two people are talking you should not butt in suddenly without saying something like, Sorry to interrupt, but. . . . And when you bump into someone it is more polite to say, Excuse me, than to glare at them. . . .'

This is the kind of advice that is of practical use, however unpalatable it may still be.

Vague language is sometimes the result of limitations of vocabulary. A woman drove into a garage and said:

'Can you help me? There's a sort of a noise thing that sounds wrong to me. I've looked, and I think the little whatsit that is usually on the top of the round thing has come off, and I am afraid it must have got into the thingmajig.'

This does not provide a very good basis for investigation.

Language is in fact rather inadequate for the expression of shades of emotion; we need at least as many words for the

43

different kinds of *love* and *friendship* as there are for the different kinds of tree in England; and we do not have them.

It is often very difficult to discuss emotions, however much we are trying to be honest. This is apt to lead to misunderstandings and unhappiness. I should think at least 90 per cent of English people—and probably people all over the world—would be much healthier, happier and pleasanter if they were told more often how much they were loved and how lovable they were. But, quite apart from any matter of shyness, of reticence, of psychological difficulties in expressing love and friendship, we very often do not have the language. 'You really are rather a pet,' says the young husband. 'You're not a bad sort yourself,' his wife replies. *Hate* too is a word that has many shades of meaning; and sometimes the shades are important. There is, I suppose, no word treating of an emotion that is not capable of being ambiguous. There are occasions when it is beneficial to keep this in mind.

Vague language is also sometimes used to confuse the reader or hearer, intentionally. 'Why must I not do that?' says one. 'Because it is not right,' says the other. 'But I see no harm in it; why is it not right?' Now, at this point a person who is trying to use words honestly at the moment has three possible replies:

1. 'Well, I don't know; perhaps it is right after all, now you ask me; why do you think it is right?'—that is, readiness to discuss the matter further.

2. 'It is not right because . . .' that, is, readiness to give a valid reason, e.g. 'because it would hurt Mary's and Martha's feelings,' 'because it will be breaking a promise . . . ' and so on.

3. 'I am afraid you will have to take my word for it at the moment that it is not right; but just now I can't explain' —an unsatisfactory state of affairs, but one that is sometimes genuine. Whether or not it satisfies the recipient will depend very much on previous experience; if the speaker is usually

fair, honest and not too authoritative the recipient may be prepared to take the declaration on trust for a time.

When we speak not so much from clear notions of what we think is right and wrong, but from our prejudices, something like this is apt to be the reply:

4. 'How dare you set up your judgment above mine? How can a bit of a girl like you possibly know right from wrong? It is very wrong to question your elders' judgment. And if you want to do things like that, it just shows that you do not know right from wrong.'

Blah, blah, blah. As soon as we examine words of this kind from the point of view of elementary semantics, we see that they are hardly real communication at all. The purpose of this kind of language (not always the conscious purpose; more will be said about self-deception in Chapter XIII) is not to communicate; it is to prevent communication.

Politicians are generally very good at using vague language to confuse. One of the most valuable semantic exercises for those who wish to acquire some grasp of the morality of politics is to translate some vague abstract language used by a politician into concrete, detailed information. This is the kind of thing I mean.

The Leader says, and how nice it sounds:

'Our gallant troops have the situation completely in hand. All of them have done their sacred duty with courage and enthusiasm. The seditious and traitorous elements who were disturbing the peace in our beautiful capital have been wiped out or rendered harmless. Our beloved citizens may once again walk in the streets, shop and go about their business in peace. And the peoples of other countries can see that only a handful of sedition-mongers are discontented; the real Utopian people has complete confidence in its government.'

As soon as we begin to translate this into concrete detail it sounds rather different:

'There is blood in the gutters and there are bullet holes in the walls of the houses round the main square. The bodies of John, Peter, Ralph, Sam, Bill, Alex and Don are buried in a common grave. Agnes has been raving in hospital ever since the stray shot killed her baby Jimmy. Three wounded demonstrators are missing. We hope they are in hospital too, but screams were heard from somewhere underneath the town jail last night. Harry, Frank, Louis, Dorothy and Kathleen were arrested and their families cannot find out what has become of them . . .' and so on. A *concrete translation*, as it might be called, often makes a big difference to our whole thought about a subject.

V. LET US LOOK AT SOME WORDS

THE first four chapters of this book have already shown that saying what we mean is not as easy as it sounds and that the meaning of most words is open to doubt, depending on such things as knowledge, context, association and background. On the whole, the more abstract a word is the more likely are semantic difficulties, unless the abstract word is also a highly technical one like some terms of philosophy and the sciences.

The word *rich* has various meanings as applied to cakes, soil, foliage, colour or silks; but in its most usual sense of *having plenty of money* its meaning may vary considerably according to the position of the speaker and hearer. Is a man *rich* if he has a net income of £1,000 a year? £5,000? £10,000? To some people a net income of £500 a year is *riches* beyond their wildest hopes; to others it is actual *poverty*. A pathetic little tale is told of an African negro, who, when a missionary was trying to give him some idea of the enormous wealth and power of Queen Victoria, said, 'Could she, then, eat tinned meat *every day*?' There is another tale of a millionaire who was invited to dine at the house of an aristocratic family. The family was very proud of its massive silver napkin rings, which were beautiful pieces of antique craftsmanship. When the millionaire saw these he did not know what they were for, and had to be told. He was shocked and distressed by the poverty and squalor of a mode of life in which people saved a soiled napkin to use it again at another meal! Very few people think of themselves as *rich*; most people think of someone else as *rich*, generally with some feelings of envy or disapproval. Being *rich* is like the previously discussed having *enough* to eat; it is always defined, not by some absolute criterion, but by the standard of the group in which, at the moment, the word is used.

We will now examine some words that are open to much discussion, and whose semantic nebulousness frequently gives rise to misunderstanding, even real distress.

I. NATURAL

There are in our everyday speech 'clean words' and 'dirty words'—words which we normally use with a tone of approval and praise and words which carry the implication of disapproval. For instance, *practical* carries approval; *Continental* for many people in England carries a hint of disapproval, although in fact both words are morally neutral as far as real meaning goes. Now *natural* is almost always a clean word; it implies something good, desirable, or at any rate permissible. People who are affected or self-conscious are told to *be natural*. Here the speaker is completely ignoring the question of what is *their* nature! It is unfortunately natural, in the sense of being psychologically predictable according to observed laws of nature, that many people should be self-conscious or even affected and insincere.

We are quite often told that a person who is deficient in the ordinary human passions is *not natural*; and even that a person who does not smoke, drink alcoholic drinks or play outdoor games is *not natural*. Again, the question arises of what is *his* nature. For example, suppose a person has no *natural passions* in the sense that he does not seem capable of experiencing sexual love or lust; if he is found to be a person with defective sex glands, his 'unnatural' attitude is perfectly 'natural'—i.e. in accordance with the laws of nature.

We are often told that some forms of medical treatment are bad because they are *not natural*. It is true that modern drugs and surgery are not found in, as it were, a wild state; but the same criticism would apply to almost all present-day human activities. In the sense in which modern biochemistry, surgery or bacteriology are *unnatural*, it is also *unnatural* to wear clothes, wash regularly with soap and use perfumes, eat cooked food, eat food we have not ourselves killed or culti-vated, use spectacles, artificial teeth and limbs, warm our-selves with gas and electricity, proceed from place to place on or in anything but our own two legs or an animal, have water sanitation and polite habits about it, read, listen to the radio, watch the television or consult a lawyer instead of fighting over the limits of our estate! A fully *natural* life would be intolerable to almost every British human being today; and most of us not only would not enjoy it, but would not survive it for more than a few weeks, even days.

The word *natural* crops up over and over again in discus-sions of the ethics of sexual and married life; and it is nearly always used very carelessly. If we are to condemn as wrong everything that is not *natural*, we shall find ourselves in the very uncomfortable position that to begin with we shall have to scrap marriage itself, since all the evidence seems to be that monogamy is not *natural* to human beings and requires considerable effort from them; yet most people would agree that marriage is indeed an excellent institution in its general concept, whatever details of reform or adjustment they would wish to see. We might even find we had to scrap all ideas of restraining our sex urges at all, and that brute force and brute desire became our only criteria. The laws of nature on the whole seem to suit the animals very well; but I doubt if a creature as complicated and sensitive as the average human

49

being, and with the numerous wants of the average human being, would enjoy a genuinely *natural* sexual life. Incidentally, if the laws of *nature* were left entirely to themselves, the relatively weak men and relatively plain women, who in a monogamous society have a reasonable chance of finding some satisfaction for their *natural* needs in marriage, would probably have no chance at all. It will be seen, though I am deliberately being rather melodramatic, that as soon as we begin to use the word *natural* as a criterion in discussing sex and marriage we are going to land in a very alarming quicksand.

We are often told that it is *natural* for men to rule women, for subjects to obey their sovereigns, for children to obey (and to love) their parents, for human beings to believe in God, and so on. When we begin to consider in detail what the word *natural* means, we begin to see that these statements are more questionable than we at first supposed. There are in the world matriarchal societies; societies in which children are not particularly attached to their parents or parents to children, very democratic societies in which there is no single superior authority, atheistically based societies in which religious hunger is by no means a usual phenomenon, and so on. To use *natural* as a synonym for *approved-of-by-me* is a very misleading habit!

2. JUSTICE

In a well-known and very powerful French short story, a father shoots his own young son because the child, in a situation that was too hard for him, has betrayed someone. When the horrified mother asks what he has done, the father replies, 'Justice'. Most of us would disagree.

Justice is another of those words it is wiser not to talk about too much. Shakespeare had noticed the difficulty in the semantics of the word when he wrote *The Merchant of Venice*.

'For, as thou urgest justice, be assur'd
Thou shalt have justice, more than thou desir'st'
(Act IV, scene i)

says Portia, after she has convinced herself that Shylock is not interested in 'mercy' and wants only 'justice'. Definitions of *justice* in the mind of a speaker may range over the following—and the definitions are important: 'what the laws of the land say is correct in the set of circumstances'—and we can all think of cases where we do not think the laws of the land are fair; 'what makes the wrongdoer suffer exactly the same distress as he has caused, or rewards the well-doer with equivalent benefits'—which is generally impossible to achieve, whether or not it may be desirable—'what satisfies all those immediately concerned as just'—which is what we often have to think of in settling disputes!—'what takes into account all the various circumstances of the dispute and treats every case or person on the merits of the special case'—ideal *justice*, I suppose, but hardly achievable all the time; and, of course, on the lips of many, 'what I have always been allowed to have before' or even just 'what I want'. A lawyer's concept of *justice* will be very different from that of a schoolboy, and the idea of an unbalanced, very selfish or very immature person will differ considerably from that of a mature, thoughtful and co-operative person; but whatever the knowledge, whatever the ethical evolution of the person using the word, there will remain some doubt as to the exact significance of the word.

3. REALITY

'Reality' (and its relations *realism* and *real*) are 'clean words', rather in the same way as 'practical'. They carry the implication that the person who claims to be in contact with *reality* is practical, sensible, honest, not dreamy, muddle-headed or sentimental. One of the results of this complex of associations has been very odd; the concept of *reality* as always 'something unpleasant that must be admitted and faced'.

The reason for this is probably that most people are more ready to pretend that things which seem to them ugly or distressing, or that do not suit their theories about life, are not there, than to refuse to believe in things that please them, suit them or fit in with their ideas. Yet even this is not entirely true; we can find people, not indeed very rare people, who refuse to accept what is pleasing and cheerful, who seem to be determined to look on the most gloomy and distressing aspect of life, who appear to be as eager to be displeased as some are eager to be pleased. There are some ostrich-minded people who do need a dose of 'stern *reality*' in being made to see that disease, aggressiveness, slums, sadism, hypocrisy and the desire to rise to success at the expense of others are actual factors in human experience. But there are also people who, in order to achieve a balanced view of life, need rather to go and look at rhododendrons, young sweethearts, goldfish, nurses, sunsets, *Swan Lake* and the life of Albert Schweitzer; these are also objective phenomena and a part of *reality*.

As a matter of fact the nature of *reality* is a question of which philosophers differ very much; and once we begin to think about the meaning of the word, instead of using it just as a 'clean word' to tell someone else to be 'practical', we find that there are more difficulties than we had supposed. For example, which has more claim to be *reality*: something that exists in my own mind, or something that, so far as my imperfect senses and information tell me, exists in the outside world? Most people who are not philosophers would probably say that the sparrow is more real than my consciousness of the sparrow; but is it? (I do not myself make the slightest claim to know the answer.) Is there any reason to think that things we find wrong or unpleasant are in some way more *real* than things we find pleasant or desirable? Are emotions real? That to anyone who has felt emotions at first sight seems a silly question; but people not infrequently use *real* or *reality* in a way that suggests that emotions are not *real.* Emotions are very *real* factors in life: for example, most industrial and political disputes are hard to solve chiefly because emotions are also involved (e.g. nationalism, memories of the past); much human conduct that at first sight appears wildly self-harming may be accounted for by emotions; and also many of our best actions in an objective sense are prompted by emotions. Suppose we act under the influence of emotions that are based on a mistake, e.g. Othello kills his innocent wife believing her to have been false to him; a man is lynched on a false charge; a war is started owing to a misunderstanding of someone's intentions; what is *real* in these cases and what is *unreal*? The emotions, for instance, are *real* as phenomena, but in another sense they are *unreal,* in that they are aroused by mistaken beliefs. And so on and so on; it is easier to tie ourselves up in the problem of defining *reality* than to solve the problem; so it may be as well not to go about talking of *reality* and *realism* as though everyone knew what they were.

4. HONOUR

There are all kinds of side meanings to the word honour, as in *Birthday honours, Honours degree, do the honours* (offer hospitality); *my word of honour* and so on. Let us take just the sense of *my personal honour.* This is a kind of mixture of *my good reputation,* especially for being (a) honest in my dealings, (b) brave, (c) loyal, (d) truthful, and, in a woman only, chaste, but this we will ignore for the moment; and *my good conduct* in these matters. Now, *honour* is certainly a 'clean word'; but for different people the criteria of what is *honourable* differ enormously. For instance, to some people it is never *honour-*

able to tell a lie, except perhaps to the enemy in wartime or to save someone else from grave harm; to others it is very *dishonourable* to tell a lie within one's particular group, but perfectly *honourable* to lie to people outside the group. In some societies and groups *honour* has much more to do with possessions, gifts and hospitality than in others; for example, there are people in parts of Yugoslavia whose *honour* is seriously offended by a refusal of an invitation, and whose *honour* obliges them never to receive a gift without giving one. To many people *my honour* is a thing that I alone am responsible for; but to many other people *my honour* can be injured, not only by my own bad behaviour but by the slanders of others. I have myself heard a very fine man say that as an *honourable man* he did not propose to make any attempt to punish some persons who had slandered and insulted him; he clearly felt that to associate with such people even by entering into conflict with them would be to stain his own *honour*, and, further, that the *honourable* man is *magnanimous* and does his best to ignore the misdeeds of pettier people. In past centuries—and it is even true of many people today—*honour* was thought of as violated if a man allowed another man to slander or insult him and did not immediately attack his insulter, either nowadays by legal means or in the past by challenging him to a duel. Those who saw the fine James Dean film *Rebel without a Cause* will remember the boys to whom *honour* (in American idiom, not being *chicken*—in British idiom, not being *sissy* or *soppy*!) involved a readiness to perform acts which were criminal, dangerous and also useless. This concept is not unusual, especially among school-children and adolescents. Moreover, we all know by experience that one person will say 'I give you my word of *honour*!' as a formula to obtain some concession and with no sense that it means anything at all, whereas to another person *my word of honour* has almost the force of an oath in a court of law—a promise that he regards as binding and indeed in a sense sacred. '*My honour* is at stake!' has spurred many people to noble and magnanimous actions, to curing their faults and to dignified self-defence; it has also driven many people to stupid angers, to needless reckless-nesses and to futile, even fatal gestures. So what the word really means is quite important.

Then, too, to some people *honour* ('clean word') is *old-fashioned* ('dirty word') and is associated only with outmoded manners and with priggishness or superstition. I leave it to the reader to think out the semantics of that.

5. MAKE A MAN OF

In so far as this phrase is not totally meaningless, since every human being who is not an unlucky medical freak is born either male or female and the male babies will, if they live long enough, become men, it has really two separate sets of associations that give it two different meanings. The idea of *man* carries in this phrase the idea of those attractive moral qualities that (rightly or wrongly I do not regard myself as qualified to say) are held to be most conspicuous or most important in the male sex: namely, courage, endurance, initiative, responsibility, leadership and dignity.

Thus when a probation officer, a headmaster or a good Army officer wants to *make a man of* Claude, he is thinking that he wants to induce Claude to be more courageous, to be more stoical in enduring discomfort or danger, to show more initiative, to take more responsibility, to prove his fitness for leadership and to have dignity in his general behaviour. He will set about this perhaps partly by rebuke and encourage-ment, exhortation, psychological assistance; he will also pre-sumably try to provide Claude with suitable company, bring him under suitable influences, cajole or force him to take part in sports and other activities requiring these good qualities, present him with difficult situations to test him and give him opportunities and so on. Claude will probably not like this; but the eventual result may make him happier as well as better. The details of the process and the question of how far such discipline should go are both very much open to argument; but the general wish to *make a man of* Claude in this sense seems to be a proper enough wish.

Yet it is not at all unusual for people to use *making a man of* in a sense which they would probably regard as the same thing—*making Claude into what it is proper a man should be*; and many people would not only seriously question, but absolutely deny, the desirability of the process. It is not uncommonly practised on young men who go into the armed forces in various countries, or into factories. This *making a man of* someone implies: getting him into the habit of swearing; teaching him to drink alcoholic drinks and, moreover, to get drunk; to smoke and perhaps to spit; to prove his 'manhood' in casual, loveless sex relations; to ignore various questions of ethics; to avoid work, to 'get away with it'; to perform various small dishonesties that are supposed to be clever; to be rude to his parents, or the women of his household; and to do dangerous things that serve no purpose. A well-known example of this odd concept of what makes a *man* is that police and doctors are generally agreed that all motor-cyclists should wear crash-helmets as a precaution in case of accident, the human head being a part of our body that we cannot manage without and that is particularly vulnerable in motor-cycling accidents. Over and over again I have heard of young men not liking to be seen in a crash-helmet because their friends would think them 'soft'! Alas, it is the human skull that is soft in comparison with asphalt or telegraph poles, and because of this vanity many young and enjoyable lives have been cut short.

Making a man of is rather like *sporting* or *a good sport*; depending on who uses it, it may range from something very valuable and sensible to something which many people would regard as downright evil and nobody, after reflection, could call desirable.

6. IMMORAL

Some of the words discussed above are weakened by the multiplicity of possible meanings; the word *immoral* has been weakened and even made a little ridiculous by extreme specialization. It originally means the opposite of *moral*: that is, *not in accordance with the principles of morality*. Now, what *exactly* are the principles of morality is not definable except within a particular church, country or social group; but in England most of us would agree, at least in general and with some reservations on points of detail, that it is *right* to work hard at our job, to help people, to speak the truth and keep our word, to be faithful to our mate, to be willing to compromise in disputes, to consider the rights of others; and that it is *wrong* to kill or hurt another person on purpose, to steal, to break promises avoidably, to do obvious injustices, to go about being rude and intolerant, to take more than what appears to be our fair share of things or to be lazy in our daily work. *Morality* covers all aspects of behaviour and, unless we belong to some absolutely authoritarian church or political party that lays down definite and rigid rules for our behaviour in all possible situations, we often have to think what precisely is indeed 'in accordance with the principles of morality'.

For what are probably extremely complicated psychological and sociological reasons, connected with a psychological tendency which I should call 'puritanism' were it not that *puritanism* is another word whose range of possible meanings is so great as to make it rather unhelpful, in England *immoral* has come to mean, for a very large number of people, only *contrary to the principles of morality in the sexual sphere*. The situation is made more awkward by the fact that there is probably no field of human life in which there is more controversy among well-intentioned and well-informed people as to what exactly *the principles of morality* are. Even what we take for granted as usual in this field, let alone what we think is right, may vary enormously with social group, standard of education, church, psychological and medical knowledge and—perhaps most of all—personal observation and experience. The result tends to be that for probably a majority of English people *immoral* means no more really than *behaving sexually in a manner of which I personally do not approve*. Indeed, the frequent use of the word is nowadays as likely to be evidence of a censorious and intolerant nature, or great ignorance of problems, as of a serious and thoughtful concern with *morality*—probably more likely. If I said 'I am afraid he is a most *immoral* schoolmaster; you can tell from his facial expression that he takes pleasure in beating his pupils', most people would be startled at the use of the word; and if I went so far as to say of a 'respectable' spinster: 'She is one of the most *immoral* people I have ever known; she is always assuming the worst of others and talking about their sins, and she makes a regular habit of discouraging young people who are trying to achieve something', many people would raise their eyebrows.

One of the odd results of this limitation of the meaning of the word is that we may sometimes hear a person referred to as *immoral* because her cosmetics are too lavishly applied, her skirt is shorter than usual or her bathing costume scantier, or she is hung about rather too glitteringly with jingly costume jewellery. Another and even odder result is that, although all mature human beings at least wish to do right when they think about the matter, the word *immoral*—being associated with sexual attractiveness, which normal people wish to have, though if they are responsible they mind how they use it—

has acquired a touch of glamour and desirability, much as certain excellent perfumes have names which by dictionary meaning are repugnant and which by association are attractive: My Sin, Scandal, Primitif, Tabu, Indiscret and so on!

7. OLD-FASHIONED AND MODERN

Both these words are semantically very interesting. They are among those not very numerous words which can according to context be either strongly 'clean words' or strongly 'dirty words'. In fact we very seldom use them with any careful thought about the meaning.

Old-fashioned might be expected to be a neutral word meaning 'belonging to past times and no longer customary'; and similarly 'modern' might be expected to be a neutral word meaning 'as is usual in the present time'—the scope in time of the words varying according to the context, for example *Modern English* is regarded as beginning in about 1450, whereas a *modern evening dress* is not likely to be more than a few years old. Yet here a psychological fact intervenes. In all of us there seem to be two opposing tendencies, though in most of us one generally predominates: a desire to be 'up-to-date', to move forward, to progress, to leave the past behind; and also a desire to look back or to go back to some Golden Age in the past. Young people are usually more 'progressive' and elderly people more 'retrogressive', but this is to over-simplify. Perhaps the two tendencies reflect the desire to grow up and be more independent, and the wish to revert to childhood or even pre-natal life in which we were more secure; in which case the predominance of one or the other wish in us will be conditioned partly by our earlier experiences and by whether our own lives have grown happier or less happy.

Old-fashioned mint humbugs and a *quaint little old-fashioned town* are Golden Age associations: we are meant to think that the sweets are made from a proved traditional recipe and from good, genuine materials; the town is thought of as pretty, quiet and idyllic in atmosphere. *Our new·modern railways* in a travel brochure carries progressive associations: streamlining, speed, cleanliness; *a modern outlook* usually, though not always, implies tolerance and up-to-date knowledge; *a modern foundation garment* is invariably a 'clean' use of the word, suggesting that the garment has been designed after recent research and with the best available materials.

On the other hand, *an old-fashioned bathtub* suggests an elaborate design and a lack of convenience that strike the present-day speaker as comic; 'You have a lot of *old-fashioned* ideas about what a girl ought to be!' is hardly complimentary in tone; and *an old-fashioned look* is a phrase sometimes used to signify a very hostile and disapproving look. Meanwhile *one of these modern girls* or *nasty modern ideas* carries a tone of strong disapproval, though the precise fault in the girls or the ideas could be defined by context only. *Modern art, modern music* and *modern poetry* are often treated as mere terms of ignorant abuse carrying the assumption that these are bad or meaningless, and are almost always terms used very loosely at best. And so on until the careful listener or reader is tempted to wonder whether these words mean anything at all.

The trouble about these words that have acquired special meanings or very loose, vague meanings that are little more than emotional noises, is not merely that they tend to confuse our thoughts. The worst danger is that they can so easily become substitutes for thought; and when we have a handy substitute for thought we generally stop thinking.

VI. WORDS THAT HAVE
CHANGED

ANGUAGE, like anything else that depends upon human beings, changes considerably with the passage of time. One result of this is that when we read the literature of several hundred years ago we are likely to be misled by words that have changed their meaning since the book was written; and sometimes much more recent writing contains a few words to which this has happened. Indeed, changes in the meaning, especially the associations, of words are sometimes so rapid that they contribute to difficulties of understanding between two generations.

This is one reason why the classics of English literature, especially the works of Shakespeare, often have to be printed with explanatory notes; unfortunately the explanatory notes often look very uninteresting and arouse suspicions that the book is going to be dull.

A person who is able to read Old English is not likely to be misled by these historical changes, since the language is so unlike Modern English that he knows he has to look in the dictionary very frequently; a person reading, say, Chaucer's Middle English or Henryson's Middle Scots is aware that he will need the glossary and will expect words to have, often, unfamiliar meanings; but when we are reading Shakespeare or later authors we often misunderstand because we are not looking for changes in meaning. The misleading word is the one that looks the same as the one we are used to and that, in the context, could reasonably mean what we at first sight suppose. For example, in *Macbeth* Ross says, speaking of the misery of Scotland under what would nowadays be called Macbeth's terror régime,

> '. . . where violent sorrow seems
> A modern ecstasy;'
>
> (Act IV, scene iii.)

If we take the words *modern* and *ecstasy* as having their present-day meaning, this makes perfectly good sense, though it is figurative: 'Where violent sorrow is the joy we have today'. This, as an indictment of a tyrannous government, is quite good. However, when the play was written *modern* meant 'ordinary', 'everyday'; and *ecstasy* had not been fixed in its present-day meaning of 'very great joy verging on an abnormal state of mind' but could mean any kind of 'frenzy', 'madness', 'mental confusion', even, sometimes, a 'faint'. Thus the 'modern ecstasy' implies: 'today violent sorrow is just an ordinary bewilderment' or something like that.

Words may have changed owing to changes in knowledge; for example, an *element* today can be strictly defined scientifically, and the elements are numerous; in Shakespeare's day the *elements* meant earth, water, air and fire.

The request in the Book of Common Prayer, '*Prevent* us, O Lord, in all our doings . . .' sounds rather odd to present-day ears, implying a request to God to hinder us from doing whatever we wish to do. Not 'in all our wrongdoings', which would make sense, but apparently in all our activities; the explanation is that when the Book of Common Prayer was written *prevent* was often used in the sense of 'go before' (from *praevenire*) and so 'to go before to protect or provide'.

John Knox's '*Monstrous Regiment* of Women' did not mean a horrifying large number of females; it referred to *govern-*

ment by women, which John Knox regarded as *unnatural*.
There is a book of narrative poems called *A Mirror for Magis-trates*, which was published in 1559. *Magistrates* here does not
mean *Justices of the Peace* or *Police Magistrates* or *Stipendiary
Magistrates*; it means *rulers* such as kings and emperors. *Sad* in
the sixteenth century often meant merely *serious*: 'Do you
speak this sadly?' meant no more than what would be meant
nowadays by 'Are you pulling my leg?'

In much more recent times a favourite hymn had a verse
which nowadays it is difficult to sing without an inappropriate
smile:

> 'They climbed the steep ascent of heaven
> Through peril, toil and pain:
> O God, to us may grace be given
> To follow in their train.'

Train of course means their *escort*, their *followers*; but nowa-days, on a mountain such as Snowdon, some choose to climb
the steep ascent with great efforts, while the weaker or lazier
members of the party do indeed prefer to—follow in the
train drawn by a locomotive. The hymn ('The Son of God
goes forth to war') is a fine one and the change of meaning
is nobody's fault; but it is unfortunate.

Matron, from the Latin *matrona*, once carried ideas of great
dignity and nobility of character, because of the high stand-ards of the Roman *matrona* such as Lucretia, Brutus' Portia,
or Octavia; it was a word for a responsible, dignified, in-fluential and virtuous married woman. Of recent times the
word has become confined almost entirely to the *matron* of
a hospital or school, who is certainly responsible and in a
dignified position, but of a different kind; so that the word in
old contexts often sounds rather odd to the reader who is
more accustomed to the new context; and with the introduc-tion of *matron* as a classification for a size in dresses not

associated with beauty or grace, the word has lost some more of its old majesty.

It may be interesting to examine a few of these words that have changed their meaniing, in rather more detail.

I. NICE

Today this is one of the most meaningless and corrupted words in the English language, an adjective of praise that saves us the trouble of thinking of a more apt word. We have a nice girl, a nice book, a nice pudding, a nice house, a nice garden, a nice cat, a nice little business, a nice sum of money . . . until the word is no more than an approving noise. It survives in one more accurate and meaningful sense in such phrases as *a nice point* or *a nice distinction*—'a point, or a distinction, requiring discrimination to decide. . . .' I have known a comic effect achieved in a mock trial by the judge's stroking his nose meditatively and saying, 'That's a nice point, that is, a very nice point . . .' where we were meant to take the word in the loose and the exact sense simultaneously.

Nice, however, was not always so vague; and its meaning has undergone drastic changes. It is actually connected with something not at all 'nice' in the present-day sense, the Latin *nescius*, 'ignorant'! In 1560 it meant *foolish, stupid*; in 1606 it was used to mean *wanton* (in the sense of *lascivious*); also in the sixteenth century it was sometimes used to signify *rare* or *strange*, *difficult to please*, *fastidious* and thus *precise* or *particular* as in the same scene from *Macbeth* previously quoted:

> O! relation
> Too nice, and yet too true!

Shakespeare also uses the word more than once in the sense of *trivial, unimportant*:

Words that have Changed

In such a time as this it is not meet
That every nice offence should bear his comment.
Julius Caesar, Act IV, scene iii.

The meaning now found in *nice distinction—requiring precision, accuracy or minuteness*—is recorded as early as 1513; and in 1586 it is recorded as meaning able to make such distinctions —*finely discriminative*. The use of *nice* as meaning 'pleasant' seems to occur first in 1713 with reference to food: *dainty, appetizing*. By 1769 the vague *agreeable* sense is recorded, and in the nineteenth century the word has come to be applied also to character: *kind, considerate*. So the development proceeds until a word which once had several, but definite, meanings has almost lost its meaning.

An interesting further development of *nice* is that it is now very often used in an ironical sense: 'This is a *nice* state of affairs!' never means what it says, but quite the reverse: 'This tablecloth is nice and dirty, isn't it?' There is also the polite use of 'not *nice*' to denote something thought of as vulgar, coarse or improper.

2. SILLY

This word now means *foolish* and is so debased that it is thought of as a little slangy or vulgar. To tell someone not to be silly almost implies that they are not only foolish but childish. Yet the word is related to the Old English *saelig*, 'holy', and did not originally carry any idea of *foolish* or *despicable*, but merely of *poor, helpless, simple, ignorant, unsophisticated*. *Silly shepherds* are found so often in sixteenth-century literature that the uninformed might be pardoned for supposing that sixteenth-century shepherds were proverbially brainless; in fact they were merely *simple* and *innocent*. (Incidentally the word *simple* has sometimes been used to mean *stupid* and *ignorant*, or even *mentally deficient*; nowadays this is a dialect or vulgar use.) Milton's

> Perhaps their loves, or else their sheep,
> Was all that did their silly thoughts so busy keep.
> *(Ode on the Morning of Christ's Nativity)*

does not mean that the shepherds' thoughts were foolish, but that they were not profound or learned. From the *poor, simple, helpless, humble* senses the idea of *foolish* developed and the word was used in this sense, but not exclusively in this sense, by the middle of the sixteenth century. Gradually the word lost its non-derogatory senses and became a word meaning only *foolish* and a very insulting word to use in seriousness.

3. TABBY

I have stressed that abstract words are more likely to be ambiguous than concrete words, but some concrete words have had great changes of meaning in the course of history. The word *tabby*, nowadays either a word for a kind of cat or a technical term used in weaving, has an extraordinary history: it is thought to come from the Arabic through Latin and French and to be connected thus with '*attabiy*, a part of Baghdad in which a particular kind of silk was made. First it was this material, with a pattern of stripes, though later the term was extended to cover other silks that were waved or watered. Then the word took other senses by analogy, to describe various other things that were striped in something the same way as the famous silk: a brindled *cat* in 1774; *moths* with this type of marking in 1819; and a kind of *concrete* that had various colours in 1802. As early as 1748 the word is also recorded as referring to a gossippy, disagreeable *old lady*!

Words that have Changed

4. DEMOCRACY

After this interlude to enjoy something trivial, let us turn to a word of immense importance today, *democracy*. It is assumed today and has been assumed for some time that *democracy* is a 'clean word', that it is desirable, worth defending, preferable to autocracy, oligarchy, or other distributions of power. I may add that I heartily agree; but the word has changed its real meaning considerably in the course of history.

The word originated in Greece with a combination of the words *demos*, 'people' and *-kratia* from *kratos*, 'rule', and in some form is now very widespread in European languages. It would naturally be rendered as 'government by the people'. But the Greek *demos* is not nearly as sympathetic to the common people as the English *people*; and the idea that government by the people was desirable or rational came relatively very late in history. This, for instance, illustrates the seventeenth-century semantics of the word:

> . . . still depending on the crowd,
> That kingly power, thus ebbing out, might be
> Drawn to the dregs of a democracy.
>
> JOHN DRYDEN, *Absalom and Achitophel*

Clearly to Dryden democracy was the rule of the rabble. The word gradually became less derogatory, very possibly as the 'people' became more educated and elections more dignified, until in 1917 President Wilson of America could say 'The world must be made safe for democracy.' This very successful and much-quoted slogan would have sounded to Plato perverse and mad.

At present it is customary to refer in non-Communist Europe and the United States to 'the democracies' meaning these countries; but the Communist countries refer to themselves as 'the people's democracies' and do not regard the Western countries as 'democracies'. I doubt if really the 'people', except possibly in Iceland and Switzerland, which are small enough, really exercise enough control over affairs in any country of Europe for it to be truly described at present as a 'democracy'. As a last shift in meaning, the word has been so much misused in propaganda activities that from a very 'clean word' it is sliding into being a 'dirty word' that can be used only ironically or with a rather apologetic air.

5. CLERK

Today this word, except in a few special administrative titles, means 'a person doing written work, accounts and so on (nowadays typing more often than writing) as an employee in an office'. The word has changed its meaning almost completely. Closely related to *cleric*, the word when first used in England meant a *clergyman*, a *churchman*. Since at one time the Church was the chief source of learning, the word came, easily enough, to mean *someone who could read and write*; and it will be fairly obvious how this could become 'office worker'.

Words also frequently change their associations for reasons of social change; some examples have already been given in Chapter III. A few more examples may be considered here. Until fairly recently in history there was nothing embarrassing or disgraceful in being bitten by a *flea*; the word was neutral until standards of hygiene and housing made fleas unusual. John Donne in the seventeenth century was able to write a witty poem about a flea that had bitten both his lady and himself; it is difficult to read it aloud today without provoking, at least for a moment, a giggle Donne would not have understood. The name of something now obsolete, such as *stage-coach* or *hansom cab*, *doublet* or *crinoline*, must now have quite a different set of associations than it had for someone to whom one of these things was visible daily and was taken for

68

granted. Progress in astronomy has given *earth, sun* and *galaxy* different associations; and *the music of the spheres*, once regarded as a fact, is now a beautiful metaphor that we can appreciate at all only with the aid of a footnote. *Heaven* and *Hell* have really changed their meanings enormously as theology has evolved. *Quaker* and *Methodist* were both once disrespectful nicknames and are now respectable, often indeed honoured terms. *Farmer* is acquiring a different set of associations as farming becomes more scientific. *Operation* is losing many of its associations of fear and peril. The word *enthusiasm* was a 'dirty word' in the eighteenth century, with associations of religious fanaticism and eccentricity; yet it is derived from a Greek word meaning 'possessed by a god' and is again today a 'clean word' such as does us good when it appears in our testimonials or is otherwise regarded as one of our characteristics.

Lemur was once known only in its mythological sense of the 'spirits of the dead', as in Milton's 'The Lars and Lemures moan with midnight plaint'; now it is known almost wholly in the sense of the charming animal of that name. *Potato* has become rather dull in its associations now that it is the commonest vegetable; in the sixteenth century its associations were luxurious, exotic and slightly disreputable. *King* and *Queen* have changed their real meanings with the decline of absolute monarchy and the development of constitutional monarchy. Distances have appeared to shorten as transport has become faster. The real meanings of the names of political parties have fluctuated a good deal more than their leaders and propagandists would often care to admit. As weapons have become more impersonal and more drastic *war* has been stripped of all its romantic, chivalrous associations; Othello's '*glorious war*' now sounds a mad combination of words. *Mill* was once a mill for grinding corn, usually a windmill or a watermill; for the last hundred years or so it has been more likely to be a cotton mill. Until the eighteenth century *nervous* meant *strong, sinewy*; it is never used in this sense today unless metaphorically with regard to literary style.

Words, then, change in the course of history, which is why great works often need uninviting little footnotes. Geography as well as history plays its part in limiting the meaning of words; as soon as we try to work with two or more languages semantic problems are multiplied dramatically.

VII. INTERNATIONAL SEMANTICS

A HUNDRED years ago the fact that different languages were spoken in different parts of the world inconvenienced only a minority. Most of those who wished or were obliged to go abroad, except in war, were people who had the money, the leisure and the cultural background to learn several major languages. Moreover, the education of the rich was then so much based upon Greek and Latin that the learning of other languages must at least have seemed easier. Today the language barrier is felt far more widely. Most English people have at least some hope of a holiday abroad at some time; trade and cultural exchanges are of increasing importance, and British firms have sometimes lost business, for example, by not giving instructions for the use of some machine in the language of the importing country. Still more important, the problem of somehow preserving peace and promoting active co-operation in the world has become the greatest problem of our time, since all other progress, survival itself, depends on this.

English people who have not been abroad, or who have travelled only to large towns and conversed only in the best hotels and the tourist shops, may say that 'someone always speaks English when you are abroad'. This is very far from being my experience. If we are to travel abroad without embarrassment and to see more of a country than can be seen by staying in a hotel that is very like an English one, we still have to solve the language problem. The Frenchman who visits England is very lucky if he can find someone who can speak French really usefully to advise him, although French is taught in nearly all our grammar schools. The Scandinavian has even more difficulty, although the Scandinavian countries have long been friendly neighbours. The Yugoslav, the Bulgarian, the Rumanian, the Pole have virtually no prospect of finding someone who speaks their languages without making special arrangements—very likely with an exiled fellow-countryman or a professional linguist.

I myself am an enthusiastic traveller and have found Esperanto, the international language, perfectly adequate for all purposes, whether to ask if I may hang my stockings up to dry or to discuss psychological research; but one has generally to arrange in advance to meet fellow-Esperantists; the fact that relatively few people learn the international language is unfortunate, but must at present be accepted. So language barriers still exist.

Anyone who has ever tried to learn a language will agree, more or less ruefully, that this is a difficult task. The mere bother of learning to call what we have been brought up to call a man an *homme*, dog, *chien*, house, *maison* and so on through all the words we expect to require, is an enormous labour. The irregularities and exceptions of the grammars of nearly all national languages greatly complicate the task, as anyone who has struggled with French irregular verbs or German strong verbs will at once admit. Swedish has one of the easiest grammars in Europe; Italian perhaps the easiest rules of pronunciation; both have maddeningly awkward difficulties in the way of saying a simple *you*, from the point of view of the English learner. Esperanto is the easiest of all languages to learn, since it was deliberately designed to be easy; but even in Esperanto the Englishman has to learn to call man *viro*, dog *hundo*, house *domo*; so considerable mental effort is still required.

International Semantics

The worst problems with foreign languages, however, are those of which we are scarcely aware at first. As soon as we enter the field of international semantics we are confronted with the difficulty that *equivalents are often not exact*. Even a large dictionary may conceal traps for the unwary.

The inexperienced student of a language begins by making obvious howlers, guessing the meaning of words from a resemblance to English words. It is very pardonable to translate *chair* in French as *chair* in English, but the French word means *flesh*. A Swede learning Hungarian and seeing the word *apa* would naturally suppose that it meant *monkey*, but in Hungarian the word means *father*; *Rock* in German does not mean *rock* in English, but English *coat*; *morbido* in Italian does not mean *morbid* in the English sense, but *soft*. Words that do not look the same, but sound much the same, also cause confusion in the spoken language; when in 1956 some young Hungarian refugees were entertained in a college and the students tried to teach them the names of common objects in the room, the word *chalk* caused a burst of laughter, since it resembles, in sound, the Hungarian word *csók*, a *kiss*!

Later the student realizes that guessing is dangerous, and learns to check meanings in the dictionary before deciding what they must mean. Yet the dictionary is not wholly reliable. There is the well-known story of the schoolboy who, working his way painfully through a French text, found the sentence: 'Rose émue répondit . . .' and turned it, by sincere but not very intelligent use of the dictionary, into 'The pink emu hen has laid another egg!' A quite good French speaker wanted to explain that he had just seen laundresses washing clothes with a *beetle* (the wooden bat used for thumping the dirt out of clothes), realized he did not know the word, tried his pocket dictionary and came out with the word *escarbot*, which does mean *beetle*, but the kind that runs across the path and has six legs. Travelling in Sweden with a camera and a very small dictionary, I asked in a photographer's shop for *lökar*, which does mean bulbs, certainly, but usually onions and in any case bulbs that one plants in the garden; *glödlampar* were what I wanted for taking indoor photographs. The lady crossing the German frontier who told the porter to carry her case into the *Gebraüche* puzzled him greatly; she wanted the *Zoll*, but both words in English have to be rendered as *customs*.

Howlers are a great source of joy and very seldom a cause of real disaster. Though they do not contribute to international understanding in the intellectual sense, they are quite likely to contribute something to international goodwill. More dangerous traps are those which are less obvious and into which even someone with a fairly good knowledge of the language may fall. The two words do in one sense mean the same; but the associations are very different, or there is a shade of meaning between the two. French *correct* applies to conduct—*proper, conventional*—much more often than it does in English. A Swedish-English dictionary will translate smörgås as *sandwich*; but the Swedish item consists of a single slice of buttered bread heaped with fish, meat, salad, etc.; it is much more palatable and much less convenient to carry than the English sandwich. The Croat *kobasica* is indeed a *sausage*; but it is nothing like an English sausage in texture or flavour. Inversely, I have known a well-bred French girl say she wanted *some bloody meat*, the French *saignant* being a perfectly polite word. One does not ask a German in a stuffy room *Sind Sie heiss?* which does mean 'Are you hot?' but has an unfortunate flavour of what we mean when we say a girl is *hot stuff*! One must be careful with the French feminine adjective *grosse*, which does mean *fat* but often means *pregnant*. A word resembling the English *professor* runs through most European languages, but the precise meaning of the word varies greatly in the various languages; so does the value

74

of the academic title denoted by the word resembling the English *Doctor*.

Even when we have mastered these shades of meaning, we may be trapped by association; and this is perhaps the most interesting branch of international semantics. An example which has caused much misunderstanding is the word *socialism*. It does not appear to present many difficulties: like many semi-technical words, it is international in form:

> French *socialisme*, German *Sozialismus*, Swedish *socialism*, Italian *socialismo*, Hungarian *szocializmus*, Serbo-Croat *socializam*, Spanish *socialismo*, Portuguese *socialismo*;

but there is often an extremely important difference depending on historical factors: in England, France, Germany, Scandinavia, *socialism* refers to the gradual, legal and constitutional introduction of changes in the economic system, the socialists being those who belong to the group known as *Labour Party* in England and *Social Democrats* in many other countries. In Russia and all countries under Communist régimes, *socialism*, instead of being sharply differentiated from *communism*, is used as a synonym, and we hear of *socialist construction*, *socialist realism* and so on. To a Western European *Social Democrat* is quite a usual and respectable thing to be; to a Communist it is a term of abuse. The meaning and associations of the word *bourgeois* (another fairly international word) vary for Communists and non-Communists; to a Communist a *bourgeois* is a rich employer of labour, which to him always implies also an unethical exploiter of labour; a French bourgeois is a comfortable middle-class person (unless the speaker is a French Communist!); the word is rarely used in English, but when it is used it generally carries more the sense of cultural inadequacy than of class or economic function. To a Russian Communist it is a term of violent hostility; to an English art student it is a mild 'dirty word' with about the same flavour as *old-fashioned*.

Associations vary for less complicated reasons. *Vin rouge* in French has as its English dictionary equivalent *red wine*; but *vin rouge* is in France one of the cheapest and most usual drinks, whereas in England *red wine* carries associations of some degree of luxury or celebration. *Meat* is an emotionally colourless word to an English speaker who is not a vegetarian; the word for *meat* in some African dialect may be charged with the powerful associations—of great luxury, of festivity, even of magic—that meat will have for someone who thinks it delicious but very rarely has an opportunity of tasting it. *Grapes* or *pomegranates*, *peaches*, *bananas*, are luxury fruits in some countries, commonplace in others. *My house has been knocked down* does not mean the same for a man who can in one day rebuild his house from sticks, mud and leaves, and to a man who has saved up for twenty years to buy himself a brick house with glass windows, a staircase, chimneys and all the other complications found in the average English house. *Marriage* does not mean the same in countries where marriage laws and customs differ; *wife* does not mean the same in polygamous and monogamous communities; *widow* still does not mean the same in France and in India. The *sun* and *rain* will be friends or enemies depending on the general climate. A *tiger* does not really mean the same to someone who has seen the creature only behind stout bars in a zoo cage and to someone who has seen a man-eating tiger drag a child into the jungle.

Expressions of emotion may differ in real meaning from country to country. A Hungarian writing to a Swedish lady caused a good deal of trouble by finishing his letter 'With true love I kiss your hands.' This was for him a usual, conventional way of finishing a letter written to a respected woman friend. To the woman's Swedish husband it implied a decidedly erotic relationship! I myself once caused some distress unintentionally by finishing a letter to a foreigner 'With love', a phrase interpreted at the receiving end much more significantly than had been intended. The French *Mon Dieu!* is not nearly as strong in its implications as the English *My God!* and is much more often heard among refined people. To call someone a *cochon* in French is a great deal more insulting than English *pig*. (It is interesting to notice the tremendous difference between English *you pig*, which may be quite affectionate, and *you swine*, which is almost regarded as foul language and is always extremely offensive. The gradations of this kind of language are often even very local; a word nearly unprintable and not used by people who wish to be thought decent in Northern England survives in my home town, Stoke-on-Trent, as a most harmless term, sometimes heard from the lips of quite respectable ladies!)

In many countries, for example, France and Italy, all letters, even the most formal letters of business, are concluded with elaborate and verbally very courteous sentences. English letters have very simple conclusions—'Yours faithfully', 'Yours sincerely' and so on, unless we are writing very intimate letters, when we may make up some more elaborate —but not stereotyped—formula. In some countries titles of respect or profession are much more used than in others. Thanks are more profuse and elaborate in some countries; and taboos are more or less strict. Such social habits, if misunderstood, may cause much embarrassment.

Minor misunderstandings that make us seem to be vulgar, insulting or critical when we do not mean to be, that give a wrong impression of our feelings or cause scandal, may greatly hinder happy relationships between two people of different nationality; and as the peoples of the world see more of one another in travel and conferences this becomes more important. International semantic problems, however, have the larger importance that verbal misunderstandings may add to international tension, creating fears, resentments, confusion where such things are dangerous. English *control* and French *contrôler* do not mean the same; the English word carries a meaning of 'rule over' whereas the French word merely means 'check' or 'inspect'. In 1905 the drafts for the Treaty of Portsmouth (U.S.A.) between Russia and Japan were written in both French and English, with *contrôler* and *control* used as equivalents: which was really intended, 'control' or merely 'inspection' was a very important point that gave much trouble. A not very diplomatic diplomatist more recently gave great offence by saying to some guests from another country, 'We shall *bury you*!' This was generally taken as a rude, brutal threat and was much resented. Later, however, an expert linguist was able to explain that in the speaker's language the statement did not imply, 'We shall kill you!' but merely 'We shall survive you . . .' with the relatively mild implication, 'Our way of life is more successful than yours.'

During World War One a mistake of this kind gave rise to a revoltingly gruesome atrocity story. The German High Command issued instructions that the dwindling supply of fats might be augmented by using *Kadaver*. Now, in English a *cadaver* is a corpse for dissection, and many people were led to believe that the Germans were using human bodies as industrial raw material. While it might have been argued that the slaughter of human beings was more atrocious than the misuse of their bodies, the latter violates a strong taboo among all civilized peoples. The atrocity story had a macabre success and is occasionally heard as true even today. But the German *Kadaver* does not denote exclusively a human corpse; it may be the body of an animal; and the instructions were that the bodies of the cavalry horses that had been killed were to be used for fat-making. To most people the idea is somewhat unsavoury, but it does not violate any taboo.

International Semantics

Careful attention to the meaning of words is very important in politics if such mishaps are to be avoided—even if treaties are to be kept, for people of different nationalities may understand the meaning of what they have agreed to do rather differently—and this is perhaps more so, because dishonest or self-deceiving politicians frequently use language in such a way as to cause confusion and prevent communication: calling names, over-simplification, whitewashing, question-begging, vaguely edifying language that in fact means nothing definable, meaningless promises, meaningless threats, are all, unhappily, part of the language of politics both national and —much more—international.

The mere attempt to discuss the meaning of words internationally is valuable; for when we begin to do this, we are beginning to look for truth; and as soon as we begin to look for truth, we also begin to calm down, we control our extravagant passions and we talk more reasonably. An interest in words and the study of languages both have a moral and social value, as well as being intellectually interesting. Even the most superficial attempt to replace ideas taken from headlines by sincere analysis of problems, even the most amateurish, but friendly, enquiry as to what the other person really means, is a small piece of real progress.

Note: I am sometimes asked what happens in Esperanto about international semantic problems. The answer is, I think, (a) that they continue to exist, for example the word *socialismo* retains its ambiguity; (b) but competent Esperantists, being able to discuss such things with a neutral language, and being usually rather notably conscious of language problems, generally come rather nearer to understanding and to the solution of semantic problems than those who are struggling to explain shades of meaning without an intermediary neutral language; and (c) that Esperanto words themselves will gradually become more perfectly defined, not only by use but by dictionary compilation; the first all-Esperanto dictionary is fortunately very good in definition, and an official Academy exists to solve linguistic dilemmas. I myself think that language will never be an entirely satisfactory means of communication, because human experience is very much more complex than vocabulary is ever likely to be able to provide for; but that is a pathetic feature of the general human situation.

PART II

The Misuse of Language

VIII. ADVERTISING

THE limitations of language and of human intelligence are such that we all have some difficulty in saying what we mean and all have some difficulty in being certain that we understand what the other person means. *Sincerity* in what we say cannot really be defined as perfect *truthfulness*, since we ourselves often do not know what truth is, or lack the words to express it, or know that the person to whom we are speaking can understand only something less than truth; *sincerity* in human beings as they at present are can be little more than a *genuine desire to communicate*, in contrast with a *desire to deceive*. This *desire to communicate* is what people often call *good faith* or *good will*; it is often not satisfied.

However, life is very much complicated by the undoubted fact that language is often used, not to communicate but to deceive. This is often true of political and religious propaganda, is far from unknown in the field of personal life, and is exemplified in the world of present-day large-scale commercial advertising.

Advertising has two functions. One is entirely socially useful, completely ethical and relatively free from semantic problems. This function is to inform people where something they may wish to buy can be bought, how much it costs, what it is like and so on. We all need to know these things; the total disappearance of advertising would make it much more difficult to find what we wanted for all except those who live in cities; and even they would have to wander in the streets for some time before finding a shop which sold what they were needing.

Assuming that the statements made in it are true, there is nothing whatever wrong with this advertisement:

SCRATCHEMS

21 Inky Way, Slaggyford, have a large stock of Fountain Pens, Ball Point Pens, Propelling Pencils, Writing Cases, Presentation Sets. Agents for all the well-known firms. Fountain Pens Repaired. If we do not have what you require, we will try to get it for you. Weekdays 9 a.m.– 5 p.m. Saturdays 9 a.m.–1 p.m.

Nor is there anything the matter with this:

FARUNA

for Flour, Cornflour, Semolina, Macaroni, Vermicelli, Custard Powder. We pride ourselves on pure goods of good quality at reasonable prices. We have just brought out a new line:

QUICKIE CREAMS
a time-saving cornflour sweet in
STRAWBERRY, LEMON and CHOCOLATE
flavours
A 1s. 3d. packet serves four.

Both these advertisements give genuine information that may be of use to someone, and do not make extravagant claims. An advertisement of this kind can of course *lie*; a 1s. 3d. packet of Quickie Cream may serve only three; but provided that there is no actual lie, there is nothing objectionable in the words. If I want to know where to buy a new pen, or what firm makes flour and similar products, I shall find what I want from such advertisements.

The second function of modern advertising is very different and frequently leads advertisers into behaviour which, to anyone who cares about words or truth, is unethical. This function is to *create a want*, not merely by stating that something may be bought—a deaf man may not *want* a hearing aid unless he knows that it is possible to obtain one, but he may be much happier for learning to want one, acquiring it and using it—but by playing on people's emotions, prejudices and ignorance to stimulate an artificial want. As soon as advertising moves from the *informative* function to the *want-creating* function, it begins to use language dishonestly.

Let us suppose that the firm making Kakao's Drinking Chocolate wishes to increase its sales. Now, the drinking chocolate may genuinely be good drinking chocolate: wholesome, palatable, pure, well packed and of reasonable price. If Kakao are going all-out to increase sales, it is just as legitimate to state these things as for me to state, when applying for a lecturing post, the nature of my degrees and my experience of lecturing.

HAVE YOU TRIED

K A K A O'S
DRINKING
CHOCOLATE?

We believe that it is a very good drink. Pure, wholesome chocolate, inspected weekly by our analyst. Packed in air-tight tins in hygienic conditions. Visitors to our factory are welcome without an appoint-

ment. Note our prices: 1s. 8d. half-pound
tin, 3s. 2d. pound tin, Family Size two-
pound tin 5s. 10d. If you like chocolate and
cocoa, try KAKAO's. We believe that you
will be pleased.

Again, so long as the statements are true there is nothing
objectionable here. The invitation to visitors may be bluff, on
the assumption that it suggests that there is nothing to hide
and thus makes people believe without investigating; but it
may also be quite genuine.

This is the kind of thing that is apt to happen; and it
happens with extravagant headlines, pictures and repetition
in many places:

> KAKAO's DRINKING CHOCOLATE takes
> away that tired feeling. Feel young and
> beautiful again! You will have the energy
> to play with your children and go out with
> your husband if your drink KAKAO's
> DRINKING CHOCOLATE every day.

How can a firm possibly be sure that it can promise this?
Tiredness may be caused by overwork, psychological distress,
anaemia and other physical illnesses, or an inconveniently
planned home. . . .

> People in the know
>   Smart people
>   Up-to-date people
> are changing to
> KAKAO's DRINKING CHOCOLATE
> Have You tried it yet?

This kind of advertisement appeals to our desire to be fashionable, knowledgeable and 'progressive'. It also makes us wonder if we are up-to-date in such a way that it touches not only pride but fear. Most of us feel insecure if we feel that we are 'behind the times' or 'left out of things'.

And we all know this kind of advertisement:

> 'I know Jim can do it!' said Mother. But his teachers were afraid that Jim was not going to pass the 11 plus examination.
> 'The boy is bright, Mrs. Hart,' they said, 'but he cannot concentrate on his work.'

These are the captions to interesting pictures of a crying mother, a worried-looking father, an embarrassed small boy and an interview with a sympathetic-looking but anxious-looking school-teacher with perhaps a blackboard in the background. Then another teacher, of course in a gown and carrying an impressive-looking chart with scientific formulae on it, appears in the next picture.

> 'Sorry to hear of your trouble, Mrs. Hart,' said the Science Master. 'But are you sure the lad is getting enough calories? Growing boys need a great deal of energy. Take my tip and try Kakao's Drinking Chocolate. I drink it every night myself.'

In the next picture we see Jim enthusiastically drinking a cup of Kakao's Drinking Chocolate and saying something about its delicious flavour. In the background stands a Family Size tin, and Mother is perhaps saying, 'Drink as much as you like, sonny, it is very economical.' (The punctuation of advertisements often leaves much to be desired.) The last picture shows a delighted family receiving the news that Jim is to go to the

Grammar School and, even as Father is congratulating him and perhaps promising him a bicycle, Mother *thinks* (people in advertisements always think in balloons above the head) 'But he wouldn't have done it if it hadn't been for Kakao's Drinking Chocolate.'

This advertisement now implies that a food product will help a boy to pass an examination; indeed the implication is that it was the chief factor. This easily deceives for two reasons; it is quite true that we work better on a good nourishing diet and most have experienced the useful energy-giving propertics of chocolate and glucose; and we would all like to pass examinations as easily as this chocolate adver-tisement implies, without mental effort or giving up many hours to hard work. We are told by implication that people with scientific knowledge approve of the product. An appeal is made to the natural and indeed admirable emotion of parental concern and responsibility; and the 11 plus examina-tion is a real cause of strain and concern to many parents and children, so that the advertisement attracts attention im-mediately and appeals to fear. This advertisement, given attraction by interesting pictures and something of a story, is far removed from a mere presentation of relevant informa-tion for the possible buyer. It is now the product of much psychological shrewdness, cynical imagination, and a cheerful indifference to truth or probability.

The reader will easily think of real advertisements that play upon the reader's desire for something quick and easy ('Slim without Diet or Exercises'—'Wash without Rubbing!'); to cupidity (£10,000 must be won in our new Oval Oranges Slogan Competition—buy your Oval Oranges today!); to the sex instinct—'Nobody wanted to dance with Jane until a friend told her . . .'—and incidentally the concept of sexual love conveyed by advertisements is generally shallow, cheap and unreal in the extreme, with no reference to friendship,

responsibility or concern for the happiness of another person;
—to fear, in a civilization already too fear-ridden ('Hair in
your Comb—what will you be like in two years?'—'Don't
ignore the symptoms of Squodge-Deficiency!'); to the desire
to feel oneself superior ('Our sort of people smoke Aristo
Cigarettes'—'Why did her Daughter's Husband not introduce
her?'); to gregariousness ('Make friends with Flip's Sweets!'
—'Everybody's talking about Anderson's new Seamless
Stockings!'); to ambition ('Men who want to get ahead read
Biblio Books.'—'Most top executives sign their letters with
a Porpoise Pen') and so on.

Another advertising technique is to produce a single short
and memorable slogan, often one that has alliteration or
rhyme to help memory or that is in itself something of a
quotable joke; these slogans often show more skill than truth.
A common advertising device which is perhaps outside the
realm of true semantics is the simple repetition of a name on
hoardings, in newspapers and so on. Pictures that associate
the product with beautiful women, distinguished-looking
men, luxurious homes, exciting holidays, loving caresses,
happy family life and the admiration of others are commonly
used; these devices might be called a form of non-verbal lie
or exaggeration.

Advertisements often misuse language in other ways, but
this is not the immediate concern of the present book. The
incorrect use of words; bad grammar; pseudo-scientific
language that sounds very impressive to those who have no
scientific background; ugly distortions of words and 'clever'
trade names made from combinations or misspellings of
words, often apt to set the teeth of anyone with any feeling
for words very much on edge; irritatingly childish gush and
childish repetitions; these are some of the offences against
language committed by advertisements.

Here is a fine specimen of semantic dishonesty:

Advertising

'SWITCH OVER TO STULTUS POOLS AND WIN £75,000!'

This at first sight appears to carry a truly wonderful promise; but the word *and* is used dishonestly. It ought to imply *and you will*; in fact it means *and you may*, the winning being not only not certain, but mathematically most improbable.

And here is another:

'WISE MOTHERS GIVE THEIR CHILDREN DAILY WOTTO!'

Never mind for the moment whether Wotto is a laxative, a vitamin preparation, a breakfast cereal or a milk drink; what is a *wise mother*? The people who are most likely to know, doctors and specialists in child psychology, are in doubt as to many of the details. Every mother who has any sense of responsibility wishes to be a wise mother and to do her best for her children; an ignorant woman, and especially one who feels unsure of herself, is quite likely to take the advertiser's statement at its face value: other mothers, wiser than she, are already giving their children daily Wotto. In fact the advertisement says no more than that a wise mother is a mother who gives her children Wotto; it is thus no more than an unsupported assertion. However, as we all know, unsupported assertions are more often believed than disbelieved. Indeed, they have to be; normally if a man says he is unmarried, or a Cambridge graduate, or able to mow the lawn, or to swim, or that he has a bank account in the town, we do not ask for documentary or practical proof. Ordinary people have seldom any means of checking the truth of assertions made in an advertisement until it is too late.

There are different kinds of assertion. 'Wise Mothers give their Children Daily Wotto!' cannot be justified, because it begs the question of what is *wisdom*. 'Blank's Biscuits are Untouched by Hand!' means something and may be either a true statement or a lie. The statements that cannot be justified usually appeal more strongly to our emotions, and thus are probably more successful in attracting customers, than those that may be genuine declarations of fact.

To read advertisements with a critical eye can be very entertaining; to read them with an uncritical eye is often to waste money, to undergo disappointment, and, by accumulation of impressions, to acquire some very unrealistic, psychologically unhealthy ideas about life. The habit of critical reading is not only good exercise for our minds; it can make a real contribution to our health and happiness.

IX. WHAT IS
SENTIMENTALITY?

SENTIMENTALITY is one of the greatest obstacles in the way of the honest, careful use of words: and the words *sentimental* and *sentimentality* are among other important obstacles.

For *sentimental* is a favourite 'dirty word' and is supposed to put an end to an argument. Unfortunately it is fatally easy to stigmatize all emotions of which we do not approve, or which we cannot understand from want of experience, as *sentimental*. The tone of voice in which the word is generally spoken makes it clear that this is a term of extreme contempt, possibly touched with amusement, more likely touched with malice.

Something must now be said clearly that particularly needs to be said in a book on semantics, which is a highly intellectual, rational kind of study. Emotion is not in itself undesirable, contemptible, a sign of weakness, a hindrance to success, or an immature quality. Emotion is a necessary feature of normal human experience; it is probably the biggest driving force in our lives; it is the source of our greatest joys except, perhaps, for a few very rare people who are dedicated to the purely intellectual life; to be emotional is not necessarily to be in the least sentimental. The most emotional woman I know, a beautiful and very artistic Slav with a dazzling personality, has also staggering capacities for self-control, patience and stoicism. The most emotional man I know is also one of the two bravest I ever expect to meet, and the most magnanimous. Occasionally we encounter someone whose emotional capacities have been almost completely destroyed by mental disorder or physical disease, or by exceptional circumstances —displaced persons sometimes seem totally emotionless, for example. Our usual reaction is to be horrified; these are the faces of pitiful freaks, or incomplete human beings.

Emotion sometimes has a special language of its own, which obeys semantic laws different from those of factual non-emotional communication. This will be discussed in more detail in the third part of this book; for the moment I will merely say that emotional language is by no means necessarily sentimental.

I am myself what might be called a professional intellectual; my intellect is trained to earn my bread and butter for me and I have much satisfaction in using it. The experiences of my intellect are not and have never been one-twentieth as important to me, as relevant to happiness or misery, as contributory to my total development and education, as the experiences of my emotions. I believe this to be true of most human beings, including most professional intellectuals.

Here are some of the things that some people are capable of stigmatizing as *sentimentality*:

The impulse of magnanimity towards a defeated enemy or an act of generosity to an enemy in trouble;

The readiness to make some sacrifice for a person we love or admire or for principles we regard as important;

The readiness to renounce some of our own rights for the sake of other people;

Forgiveness of those who have done us some harm, and an attempt to find excuses for them;

The capacity to feel admiration and reverence for a person obviously more intelligent, more creative, more magnanimous or in some other way of greater moral achievement than ourselves, and the desire to imitate the good qualities of that person;

The feeling of pity for persons in distress, the impulse to comfort and caress them and the impulse to perform practical actions in order to help them or console them;

The practice of commemorating important events in our lives and raising morale by celebrating birthdays, wedding anniversaries and so on;

Acts of commemoration to pay respect to those who have died in the service of mankind;

Gentleness and patience in our dealings with children, animals, the elderly, and in general those weaker than ourselves;

Respect and kindness to our parents when they are growing old and we are in the prime of life;

Attempts to promote friendly feelings and understanding between the peoples of different nations;

Attempts to suggest methods of dealing with criminals that shall aim at cure rather than mere punishment;

Attempts to protect the weaker members of society by means of various welfare schemes and social services;

The love of a parent for a child;

Friendship that includes the exchange of confidences and help and is not merely the barren acquaintanceship of bridge partners or talking about the weather;

The experience of being genuinely in love, which for millions of people is the greatest illumination that life has ever given them.

To obliterate such emotions, such actions, such experiences from our lives would not be to become rational and superior beings. It would be tragedy. It would not be the beginning of real human progress; it would be the end of all hope for human progress; it would be the beginning of the human ant-heap, the true reign of the robots. Perhaps fortunately,

What is Sentimentality?

the end of emotion would also be the end of mankind in one generation; for no more children would be born; it is even imaginable that the very will to live would cease to exist.

I was once asked what my idea of Heaven was. I could give many answers, some flippant, some abstract, some allusive; but my answer then was: 'I think that Heaven would be a state of mind in which we were all able to treat everyone else with the generosity, the charity, the understanding and the happiness in their existence that we show when we are genuinely in love with a particular person.' I am not ashamed today of this definition. Experience has so far confirmed in me the belief that what little wisdom we have is acquired mostly through our affections. It has also, on the whole, made me believe that we do well to be demonstrative and affectionate in a love-starved world, and to express freely at least those of our emotions which are not objectionable to others.

An investigation of the meaning of *sentimentality* helps us to combat this wrong use of it as a 'dirty word' to denigrate our emotions and frighten us from our tender, humane, loving or loyal impulses. In fact *sentimental* people are often not very strongly *emotional*. Strong emotions are very often found in conjunction with strong character, considerable self-discipline and high principles; those strong emotions themselves tend to provide the dynamic for character development.

Sentimentality is a *falsifying of emotion*; properly used, the word implies something essentially *unreal*. Let us take a few concrete examples. When we begin to feel sorry for ourselves, we soon become sentimental; we see our case as more pitiful than it is; we imagine how sorry for us other people would be if they knew of our woes; we also blame the harsh world for not understanding us; we begin eventually to feel the kind of glow of self-approval that would be justified if we were really suffering for the sake of some friend or some great cause. We come to feel a sort of satisfaction in our own wretchedness. Sentimentality! The realistic reaction to suffering, except in very rare circumstances (there are hopeless cases, but not many of them) is to see what we can do to remedy our distresses, not to sit down and wallow in them.

Two sisters lived together. Once a week they visited the grave of their dead brother, of whom they were very fond. One day the younger sister was seriously ill in bed on the usual day for the visit to the grave. She begged her elder sister not to leave her, being afraid that she might become worse. The elder sister argued with her, then burst into tears and said, 'You can't have loved poor dear Theodore to be so disrespectful to his memory, and you can't love me either to ask me to do such a wicked thing!'—Sentimentality. What has happened in the emotional life of the sisters is that, as it were, their scale of priorities is all wrong.

A journalist, some years ago, was astonished by the reactions of the audience at a film depicting scenes of the Spanish Civil War. Fearful scenes of death, wounds and destruction flickered across the screen. The audience sat watching with remarkable stolidity as human beings suffered, human beings, incidentally, who were often passionately devoted to principles. Suddenly the film showed an overloaded baggage donkey walking through the gunfire. A woman who had before seemed quite unmoved exclaimed then, in a voice choked with tears, 'Oh, the poor little donkey! Look!—isn't it a shame? How can people be so wicked?'

It is not *sentimental* to love or to be 'in love'. Much sentimentality often attaches itself to love, precisely because the experience is so real and so important that many of us have difficulty in coping with it. A very common form of sentimentality is the line of behaviour that may be summed up as 'If you won't do this for me, you don't love me,' or

even, 'If you don't think just as I do, you don't love me.'
Now, it is true that anything I am prepared to call *love*
includes a serious concern for the welfare and happiness of
the other person; but someone who claims that love should
mean a total surrender of the 'loved' person's will has a very
immature and very unrealistic idea of love. Love is a partner-
ship, not a swallowing. Jealousy is an emotion that I suppose
we cannot always help, though I think it is one to be restrained as far as possible; but the assertion that jealousy is a
proof of love has always seemed to me to be a very sentimental assertion, based on the sentimental premise that true
love is possessive, monopolistic. In particular, we find almost
unrelieved sentimentality in the not uncommon assertion
that unprovoked jealousy in a proof of love. The man who
finds his wife on the sofa kissing another man has a problem
to face; he is jealous reasonably and must deal with his
jealousy and his wife's behaviour as his own set of values
and morals dictate; but the man who makes a scene because
his wife has an ordinary letter from another man or is polite
to another man at a party is not showing his love; he is
showing childish possessiveness and insulting mistrust. Many
of us, behaving like this (and most of us do fall into unreasonable and childish jealousy on occasion, if not in love then in
some other sphere of life), then make beautiful excuses to
ourselves: 'I shouldn't make scenes if it weren't that I am
so much in love with you. . . .' (Liar!) or 'I am not jealous,
but I don't like her getting so much attention. . . .' (Liar!)
This is sentimentality.

It is often difficult to see at what point sentimentality
begins when we set a value higher than their market value
upon objects because of the circumstances in which we
acquired them. There is always a danger of growing sentimental over such things; probably the answer is that we
should watch ourselves and aim at keeping such feelings

under the control of our common sense. That a gift is more precious because a loved person gave it is perfectly normal and rational; that we should grieve for days because it has accidentally been broken or lost seems to be rather losing a sense of proportion.

Before we have any right to call emotional manifestations *sentimental*, except in such a phrase as 'of sentimental value', which is not a 'dirty word', one of the following three factors must, I think, be present; and usually, where there is real sentimentality, more than one will appear:

1. Some kind of *unreality* in the emotion itself. This can often be felt rather than defined. It may be found in an unreasonableness of expectation—'If you lose your temper with me, you can't possibly love me!'—'You ought never to forget that I lost my husband three years ago!'; in a want of proportion as between the stimulus and the emotion, as when someone sobs broken-heartedly for hours and makes the maid's life a misery because the maid has broken a vase the mistress liked; or when someone goes into a passion of anger and cannot be conciliated because someone has said in a good-humoured tone, 'You are a fathead!' or when someone goes off into 'You hate me!' denunciations over a mildly expressed refusal to do something; in an element of deception or self-deception which gives a feeling of play-acting (though here we have to be very careful and hesitant in our judgments, as, depending on temperament, nationality, articulateness and state of health, some people do in fact express their authentic emotions much more dramatically than others); in a very persistent refusal to listen to courteous and reasonable argument after a moderate interval in which to compose ourselves; in a prolonged repetition of some assertion or emotional gesture without developing any further or doing anything constructive; and so on.

We always have to be cautious and charitable, and should

98

be more ready to suspect sentimentality in ourselves than to denounce it in others; people of sincerity and good sense do differ considerably in their emotional experiences and reactions and generalization can be very misleading. There is a demonstrativeness that is gushing and insincere, and a demonstrativeness that is a sign of genuine emotion. There is an emotional excitability that springs from a lack of ordinary self-control and common sense, and an emotional excitability that may be combined with great self-control, the outbursts of open emotion being infrequent or well motivated. We must not go about assuming people are sentimental because their emotional behaviour does not coincide with ours.

2. An *exaggeration* in the expression of the emotion. Such violent expressions as 'I'd rather die than . . .', 'You have always been cruel to me . . .', 'I shall go mad if you don't do as I ask . . .', 'I will do anything for you! . . .' may be true, but more often they are not. When we begin to think about the meaning of words, we tend to dislike the sound of such expressions on our own lips, and to feel a desire to check their genuineness before saying them.

3. Some degree of *deliberately stimulating our own emotions further*. We all know what it is to nurse anger, to wallow in our own misery until, in a sense, we are enjoying it, to make the most of a fit of bad temper, to sulk longer than we can help in order to enjoy the embarrassment of whoever has annoyed us, to search out associations that will tend to make us cry at a stage when we might be able to restrain our grief, to make little pilgrimages and repeat actions from a desire to feel the relevant emotions again (though this may, in a few contexts, have its genuine value), to brood over the photograph of someone we love who is unattainable, and so on. A great deal of political propaganda plays upon the human capacity for enjoying our own emotions; unfortunately, one of the favourite emotions of the demagogue is

hatred, which nearly always does harm; if he aroused an artificial tenderness or an artificial desire to co-operate he might accidentally cause a certain amount of objective good.

I have tried at some length to differentiate sentimentality from genuine emotion, partly because *sentimentality* as a dirty word is politically, socially and psychologically a very dangerous one, and partly because the people for whom this book is primarily written may find this distinction a particularly urgent one. What is the effect of sentimentality on our use of words?

Exactly the same: *unreality, exaggeration* and *a use of words to whip up more emotion* rather than to achieve communication. Words such as *love, hate, angry, broken-hearted, grieved, hurt, loyalty, devoted to, adore, crazy, cruel, wicked, wonderful,* lose their proper meaning and become little more than emotional noises. Other words such as *home, flag, family, mother, son,* may be used to heighten the false or immature emotion by association. The language of sentimentality is also very often either an imitation of the language of strong emotion that has been heard in the past, or an imitation of the language in which strong emotion has been indicated in films that the speaker has recently seen. The imitativeness is part of the unreality. Another common sentimental use of language is to compare ourselves to someone to whom we very clearly do not deserve to be compared, or to compare our opponent or wronger to someone very much worse.

In the speech of sentimentality we often use our words as much to keep our own emotion alive as to communicate it to anyone else, or to make another person believe we are feeling the emotion, in order that they will have the reaction we want: will pity us, admire us, be sorry for the dreadful thing they have done to us, love us in return, be suitably grateful to us, help us and so on.

The opposite of sentimentality is, then, not *lack of emotion,* not even *self-control*—for not all uncontrolled emotion is unreal or even undesirable—but *sincerity*. In using our words, as in living our lives, we all need to consider, every now and then, whether we are really being genuine; and we must bear in mind that being fully *sincere* almost certainly implies, on many occasions, being *fair* and being *moderate*.

X. WHAT I TELL YOU THREE TIMES IS FALSE

EVERYONE who has ever learned the multiplication table, a poem, or some irregular verbs by heart knows that repetition is very important indeed in fixing information in our minds. All teachers make great use of this fact. Only very rare people (Lord Macaulay is said to have been one of them) absorb large quantities of information after simply receiving it. Most of us learn things largely by being told, or telling ourselves, over and over again. The methods of hypnosis and of those useful psychological treatments based on suggestion and auto-suggestion make great use of repetition. Thus repetition is extremely important as an educational tool.

Unfortunately this valuable tool can be misused. I can, by frequently saying to a child, 'Look both ways before you cross the road!' fix in the child's mind a habit which may save its life or limbs. I can with equal success say so often to a child, 'You are a clumsy little boy!' that he becomes incurably clumsy, a failure whenever he has to use his hands. A preacher may tell his congregation repeatedly that they should try to think charitably of their fellow human beings; and he will do at least some good; but a demagogue will be equally successful in convincing his admirers that the inhabitants of the Aleutian Islands are about to attack Canada, if he says so often enough, in spite of the extreme improbability of such an event.

What I Tell You Three Times is False

Because when we have a habit of hearing things we tend also to acquire a kind of habit of at least readiness to believe them, we can usually examine the meaning of some quite unfamiliar statement more critically than that of a statement we have often heard before. Most of us have probably had the disconcerting experience of thinking we believed something until confronted with an unbeliever who argued, and then suddenly discovering that we did not believe, that we had taken the belief on trust from so early an age that we had never examined it. If I say to a group of students or children, 'It is very wrong to squotch wogglegooks,' they will demand a definition of this mysterious misdeed and not wish to take my assertion for granted. If, however, I say, 'It is very wrong to make other people unhappy!' almost any British child or student who has been brought up in an average well-intentioned home will at once agree with the statement, and will probably not realize that *making other people unhappy* may be defined very strictly or very loosely, depending on our definition of unhappiness.

It follows that, since we are more likely to be misled by repeated assertions, precisely the assertions we most often hear are those we should examine most carefully with regard to their meaning, in order to consider whether or not they are true. Our most dangerous errors are probably the ones we take for granted.

This does not mean that something we often hear is necessarily not true, or even ambiguous. We have often been told that twice two are four; the statement that twice two are three is more original, but the commonplace is true and the daring innovation is of no value. The fact that a very large number of sane people agree on something, for example that peace is desirable, or that money does not guarantee happiness, or that a hungry man is an angry man, does not prove the truth of the statement; at one time an enormous majority of no doubt sensible people believed that the sun moved round the earth; but it is some evidence in favour of the correctness of the assertion; if a great many sane people all come to the same conclusion about something, they have at least some reason for doing so.

Two kinds of repetition that tend to make us uncritical are *slogans* and *clichés*. Slogans are, in the present-day sense of the word, which once had a rather more dignified meaning, short, memorable and impressive sentences used to summarize a political aim or to advertise some product or perhaps idea. They include such statements as 'An apple a day keeps the doctor away', which contains some measure of truth, in that apples are a healthy food, but which is demonstrably not fully true; 'Beer is best!', which does not mean anything until we know best *of what* or best *for what*; 'A fair day's wage for a fair day's work!' which is most reasonable in tone, and to which, as a principle, most people would agree, but which contributes nothing to policy, since both the *fair day's work* and the *fair day's wage* require definition; 'Vote for Putten and Prosperity!'—which implies that Putten and his party can guarantee something no single party in a single country can possibly guarantee, and leaves *prosperity* undefined— whose? when? what kind of? what level? at what cost in other things? and so forth.

The purpose of slogans is: (1) to impress by repetition and make us do what someone wants, whether something sensible —'Wash your hands before eating' or something less sensible —'Eat Blotto's biscuits and be Beautiful!' (2) to simplify what is usually a complicated matter so that it has an immediate appeal to uncritical minds. Political slogans, for example, generally make large and attractive offers, but do not give any indication of how the goal is to be reached or even how the party can be sure of reaching it; though the most magnificently unintelligent political election slogan I ever saw, which must have been making its appeal entirely to the inarticulate disgruntled, and which was in fact, I understand, quite successful, was: 'It's Time We had a Change!'. This is really clever as propaganda, though utterly stupid as argument; it leaves the disgruntled elector to imagine that a new government will be able to redress all his grievances and that all kinds of wonderful things will happen. Advertising slogans make the names of products conspicuous, so that people will select a named product in a shop when buying; but they also make encouraging generalizations. Advertisements frequently use 'clean words' which immediately sound good—'the *scientific* soap'—'the *modern* way of washing'—'the *friendly* firm to deal with'—'the drink for the *home*'—'the *latest thing* in figure control'—'the paper for *top people*' and so on.

When we stop to analyse the meaning of words, advertising and political slogans can no longer have any power over us, for they are nearly always meaningless in the true sense of *meaning*; that is, they do not really tell us anything. Then we shall, before buying a product, want to look at it, learn what we can about it, listen to what friends who use it say, and so on; before voting for a political party, we shall want at least to know something of its real programme and the qualifications, moral and intellectual, of its leaders; we shall, in short, make some attempt at making our decisions like fairly rational beings, instead of acquiring what could almost be called a set of mental conditioned reflexes to certain sounds.

Clichés are, as it were, the slogans of our everyday conversation. They are those combinations of words which we all use often without stopping to think. They do not improve the style of writers and too many of them make even ordinary conversation dull. Worse, they tend to be a handy synthetic substitute for both expression and thought.

I do not think it is possible to converse or write without

some clichés. We cannot, at least in ordinary talk, be thinking every second of exactly what we are saying; a good deal of daily talk is not aimed so much at exact communication as at making friendly, obliging noises. When two people talk for a few seconds about the weather they are not usually interested in it; it is merely a topic that will not be controversial and that we discuss to indicate a willingness to make ourselves pleasant. Possibly in some primitive society you might give me a nut and I give you an edible berry with exactly the same real significance, 'I-am-willing-to-be-friendly-with-you-and-wish-you-no-harm!' as is evident today when you say, 'Lovely weather we've had for a couple of days, haven't we?' and I reply, 'Yes, much nicer than last week.' That we often say, 'I am sorry to have been tactless!' when we are really thinking, 'You are a nuisance with your morbid touchiness!' or that we say, 'How well you look!' when we are thinking, 'I bet most of that complexion comes out of a box!' is just as well if people are to live together in something like peace. We cannot possibly, in the world as we at present know it, be on terms of close friendship with everyone we 'know'. Similarly, most of us often have to write a letter whose purpose is not really to communicate, but to show another person that we have had a kind thought about them. The traditional postcard from a holiday resort—'Having a wonderful time; wish you were here!' does not express a real longing for the company of the addressee; it is a way of showing friendliness, an expression of a desire, sincere or not, that another person should also have a wonderful time. I was once able to amuse my mother, with whom I am very intimate, with a holiday postcard, 'Having a wonderful time; just as well you are not here!'

When in our speech or writing we really are aiming not at friendly or protective gestures but at *communication*, clichés are often a great hindrance. Unfortunately it is very easy to use them as if they were final, devastating answers, either to our own arguments or to those of other people. They are expressions that we have accepted so often and for so long that we find it very difficult to question them.

'A little of what you fancy does you good.' For mature people in fairly good health this is often true, because a small treat gives psychological satisfaction and that tends to promote health and balance. The human body is normally fairly adaptable. In many circumstances the old lady who feels she wants a strawberry ice or the workman who sees and smells some fresh sausage rolls and thinks he will have a couple for tea instead of the usual sandwiches, will do well to indulge their fancies; and in the experience of many people a 'fancy' is Nature's way of indicating that we need something in our diet. (I hardly ever touch an orange except when I have a cold; then I seem to acquire an almost insatiable craving for them; and vitamin C is said to be very valuable in the treatment of colds.) But to a person just convalescing from typhoid fever 'a little of what he fancies' may be even fatal, this being an occasion on which a patient is apt to fancy very unsuitable articles of diet; and a young child not infrequently wants to eat something that will do harm.

'Mother knows best.' A good mother has, in the process of bringing up children, acquired a great deal of valuable experience, of balance, of knowledge and of inner wisdom that makes it likely that what she has to say is worth listening to. Not all mothers are wise, kind or conscientious; and not all human beings seem capable of learning much from experience. I think myself that any mother who is making a fair success of her hard and responsible job deserves a great deal of respect, especially from her children; but the mother of an atomic physicist is most unlikely to know better than he does about atomic physics, the mother of a ballet dancer probably knows comparatively nothing about her daughter's art and career; and many wise and good mothers cannot claim to *know best* about some matter affecting the lives of their grown-up children, merely because the whole set of circumstances is very different from that of Mother's time.

'Love is blind.' This is a useful cliché for sneering at people and often a useful excuse for ourselves. Is it at all true? I do not think so. There is a certain kind of physical infatuation that, for a short time, is 'blind' in the sense of being uncritical, uncomprehending, without any sense of proportion, without any patience or any forethought. It is a painful and sometimes a tragic experience. But what mature people would call love, either sexual love or some other form of love —that of mother, father, brother, sister, child, friend, for example—is often extremely realistic, shrewd, perceptive and understanding. In the happiest marriages I have been privileged to see, husbands and wives, so far from being 'blind' about one another, had an extremely detailed and subtle perceptiveness about one another. This included a capacity to perceive some faults and weaknesses; it also included a very great capacity to forgive those faults and excuse those weaknesses, as we must all forgive one another many things if we are to live together peacefully. Real, mature, responsible love is, in my experience and observation, a very important source of knowledge about people and even of wisdom.

'It'll all be the same in a hundred years!' is a wonderful cliché for excusing ourselves, for refusing to give sympathy to those in trouble and for avoiding responsibility for doing anything about abuses. It is, perhaps, one of the stupidest of all popular clichés. For life is so extremely complicated that almost any circumstance, any word, any action, may have an effect on what happens in a hundred years' time. For example, a girl today may be upset because her boy friend has grown tired of her. It is very easy to say, 'It will be all the same in a hundred years!'—very easy, that is, for someone else, who does not want to 'waste time' sympathizing. Now, suppose in her grief, anger and humiliation the girl too hastily accepts the courtship of someone else who is not really suitable, as has often happened; makes a rash marriage which turns out to be an unhappy one; and then tells her young daughter, eighteen years later, that men are horrible and selfish. The daughter, at twenty-five, marries, for, being a normally constructed human being, she is capable of 'falling in love'; but, because of psychological resistances created by the talk of her disappointed mother, she in turn becomes a disappointed and disappointing wife; and the son of her unhappy marriage is given the impression that marriage is not a good idea at all. He is determined to remain 'free'. Thinking himself a 'clever fellow' who is not going to be 'hooked', he, some fifty years after the original episode that was going to 'be all the same after a hundred years', becomes the father of an illegitimate child. This boy has a very unhappy childhood and as a result grows up with a feeling of resentment and grudge against society and a distrustful attitude towards everyone. He also puts a very exaggerated value on the usual family life that he has been denied, thinking that he would be perfectly happy if only he had had a home. Craving to be important, he goes into politics and becomes a clever speaker who knows how to play upon the unhappiness of others, the secret feeling we nearly all have that someone or other is preventing our total happiness. In middle life he becomes a dictator of the Fascist variety, chases women back into the kitchen, undoes all the good that has been done in many years by social workers and psychologists, persecutes minorities in the country, and perhaps plays an important part in starting a war. A girl's mortification a hundred years ago was a link in a chain of consequences that perhaps caused several million premature deaths and uncountable misery. I have, of course, imagined a dramatic and extreme case; but anyone who looks back on life can see occasions when something that to others seemed trivial played an important part in the history of a life; and all lives affect the lives of some other people; so any cliché that renounces responsibility may be a very harmful one.

Thus whenever we are presented with some cliché as though it were a universal truth we must immediately accept, we shall be wise to examine it.

Two other ways of winning assent to something that is not necessarily true, without having to go to the trouble of defending it, are 'taking for granted' and 'begging the question'. These dishonesties—not necessarily intentional dishonesties—are usually not so much a carelessness about the meaning of single words as a general carelessness in thinking. We tend, for instance, to take for granted in argument that: all people wish to be healthy, when many people find certain advantages in some ill-health; all women wish to marry, which is not a 100 per cent true; hot sunny weather is better liked than rainy cold weather, though a minority of people feel unwell in hot weather; work and effort are disagreeable, which is very largely a falsehood taught by the too numerous people whose work is excessive or seriously uncongenial; only children are spoilt, when in fact the parents of only children are quite often so anxious not to spoil them that they are over-strict and expect impossible standards; what does another country good does our own country harm, which in many fields of activity is the opposite of the truth; similarly, that in our own country there is only a certain amount of material wealth and that if one group receives more another group must receive less, when other economic changes may modify the amount available and so complicate the arithmetic; home life is desirable for everyone, when a few people have neither the desire for it nor the need for it; all parents do their best for their children and want their children to be happy—

which any social worker can tell us is not always true; and so on.

Much of what we are ready to take for granted is 'true' enough for our everyday purposes, in that it applies to most people in the circumstances with which we are likely to be dealing. 'Begging the question' is more truly dishonest. We cannot question everything all the time, or nothing will ever get done; but we can try to argue fairly.

When someone says to her teen-age daughter, 'You ought not to wear lipstick because it is wrong,' she is saying no more than 'You ought not to do it because you ought not to do it,' which does not contribute anything to the argument. When a politician says, 'All who truly love their country will accept the necessity of these sacrifices' he is making it very difficult for anyone to argue that the sacrifices are unnecessary, for fear of being thought unpatriotic. If someone says to me, 'I think you are being too lenient with your pupils; I would like to show you the careless work some of them have been doing lately, and to tell you what Jane, Susan and Pauline have been up to in the vegetable garden! They are getting into the idea that anything will do!' it is quite possible that she may have something to say which will modify my theories and my behaviour; if she says to me, 'All sensible people know that girls need strict discipline, and I wonder that an educated woman like you can be so stupidly soft!' I can safely take no notice of her, for her 'All sensible people . . . .' is obviously only a paraphrase for 'All people who agree with me. . . .'

'What do you think of the outrageous, wicked views of Freud?' assumes that the other person has already made up his mind to agree with the speaker. If the reply is, 'I think them neither outrageous nor wicked, but am not sure that I understand their full implications!' the reply may never be pronounced for fear of being thought 'wicked', or may be greeted with embarrassing astonishment. When people use begging-the-question arguments against us, we can generally, if we are alert, detect the dishonesty, the way in which we have been given a phrase, not a contribution to argument; when we do it ourselves or it is done in defence of something in which we believe, the dishonesty is less obvious!

I knew a charming and clever Pole whose knowledge of English was imperfect and who had a special and rather engaging technique for begging the question. When cornered in argument and unable to give a reply, but still obviously feeling that only a very perverse individual would question the truth of his first assertion, he would say, waving his hands appealingly, 'Oh, well, because *because*.' This sounded rather sweet and was well calculated to appeal to the indulgent maternal instinct.

But it was not argument. To do him justice, it was not meant to be, and was usually a signal to put the kettle on.

XI. WHITEWASH LANGUAGE

SERIOUSLY neurotic people are often apt to dislike and despise themselves and to think much worse of themselves than the objective facts would justify. The majority of human beings, however, tend to judge themselves and their families, organizations, countries and so on more leniently than they judge their neighbours, other organizations or other countries. This comes out in our choice of words. So long as we realize what we are doing it does not matter; but when we are not conscious of this natural human inclination we can be very untruthful, unfair and even dangerous by our misuse of words.

There is a joke conjugation: 'I am firm, thou art obstinate, he is pig-headed.' I would continue it in the plural as 'We are united in perfect solidarity, you people all stick together, they are an obstructive clique.' This flippancy contains a great deal of psychological and moral truth.

'I have quarrelled with Green,' says Brown, 'because I can't get him to see reason at all. What an obstinate fellow he is! And he is an egotist too; he cannot see any point of view at all except his own. Now, I claim to be a man with a will of my own. When I have made up my mind, I know what I want and I set out to get it. I don't allow anything to stand in my way; I don't shilly-shally and waste time with a lot of words; I go ahead and get it. But you can't talk to Green; he just wants his own way and nothing I say can make him see reason.'

Translation: Brown has quarrelled with Green because

Green, just like Brown, can see no point of view except his own and wants his own way!

Now, in such conjugations as: 'I pride myself on my civilized tolerance; you are rather too broad-minded if anything; he has no moral sense at all,' or 'I do know how to relax; you might put more effort into things; he is bone lazy,' or 'I am glad to say I enjoy my food; I believe you are putting on weight; he gorges like a pig!' or 'I am tactful; no one knows where they are with you; he is a slimy hypocrite!' It is not always easy to say which form of words comes nearest to the truth about the person. To add to the complications of trying to pass judgment, circumstances frequently alter cases; for instance, what may be a wise awareness of how to relax in someone just recovering from a breakdown may well be bone laziness in someone else; an active growing adolescent may have what in a man of fifty would be a hoggish appetite, and need every crumb consumed. We cannot assume that either the praise of the first-person form or the brutal criticism of the third-person form, or for that matter the moderate criticism of the second-person form, is the way we ought to think. What we ought to bear in mind is that we are extremely apt to whitewash ourselves and also to blackwash other people. 'Well, what do you want?' is not always the right reaction to a compliment; many people deliberately seek opportunities of paying honest compliments in order to give pleasure to other people and to encourage them. We are wise to remember that those who are always attributing the lowest motives to others are giving, unconsciously, a disconcerting picture of how their own motivations work.

Before examining whitewash language, the language we tend to use in speaking of ourselves, I will touch upon a point that may be helpful to some. We are all taught, if we receive any kind of moral instruction, that we should try not to be selfish, not to think too much about 'I'. This seems to me to be very sound; the more we all try to make others happy and the less aggressively we push our own interests, the more likely we are to make the world a pleasanter place. But the advice not to be selfish is often misunderstood in two ways. One is that legitimate statements of objective fact about ourselves are apt to be taken in England as 'blowing our own trumpets'—a champion tennis player is rather expected to talk to the effect that he pats a ball about a bit for fun; a very brave man, much decorated for valour, is expected, if someone like me who is not brave asks him to give some advice on cultivating courage, to disclaim any title to courage, instead of giving advice which could be useful. A rich man is supposed to pretend that he is poor, a clever man that he is stupid, a staggeringly beautiful woman that she has nothing special about her; and of course a child or adolescent is not supposed to mention *anything* meritorious he or she may have done. I suspect that this convention may lead to more misunderstanding than it prevents and may deny us all much interesting and useful information; there is all the difference in the world between noisy boasting and a matter-of-fact admission that one has done something rather unusual.

A second convention of unselfishness is that it is egotistical and vulgar to use the word 'I' avoidably. Is this true? Nobody likes a person who is endlessly talking about himself or herself and does not seem to show any friendly interest in other people or respect for their achievements; but 'I' is a perfectly respectable and necessary word to describe the person who is speaking.

'Don't know how anyone can eat cod's roe. Disgusting, revolting stuff!'

'I don't like cod's roe.'

The first is a silly over-generalization; many people are fond of cod's roe and do not find it unappetizing; the speaker implies that there is something wrong with other people's taste if they can eat it. The second speaker, using 'I', merely makes a reasonable statement of fact that may be useful to a hostess or nurse in planning meals. The same technique of avoiding the terrible taboo 'I', when carried into more important fields of activity, leads to intolerance and rudeness.

'All sensible men are agreed that we should guard our oil interests in the Middle East, by force if necessary—drop a few bombs on the blighters if they give trouble! And you will find that everyone who cares for his country thinks the same way!'

The man who says this implies that if I happen to disagree with him on grounds of morality or expediency I am a silly person, and goes on to imply that if I disagree I cannot love my country. This makes decent argument embarrassing, perhaps impossible to a shy opponent.

'I think, myself, that our oil interests in the Middle East are so vital that we ought to defend them by force if necessary. To me this is the only patriotic attitude.'

The use of the 'I' immediately leaves room for the possibility that the 'you' may think differently and has a right to do so; that the opinion expressed is held only by the 'I', one fallible human being. Surely this is in fact a more modest way of putting things than to imply that what the 'I' happens to think may be attributed to 'all sensible men'?

This careful avoidance of the 'egotistical' *I* leads some people to use *we* when they are neither royal nor editorial; to use *one* in a curiously affected fashion; to criticize and censure others as a mode of praising themselves; to make these 'all sensible people' generalizations so as not to admit that 'I believe'; and to give reasons for doing something that are not in the least genuine, e.g. 'It would do you good to have some exercise!' as a polite expression for 'I don't feel like cutting the lawn.' A little more admission that we are all selfish and all fallible and that each 'I' generally thinks first of 'me' might tend in the long run to make us less rather than more selfish, and certainly more sincere.

We may now turn to the things that 'I' tends to say about 'me'; the whitewash language whose function is to justify 'me'. The most dangerous feature of this habit, which we all have more or less, is not that it deceives other people; very often it does not; but that it helps us to deceive ourselves.

Bill gets drunk. This can happen to anyone. If Bill's subsequent attitude is: 'I got drunk; that was foolish and dangerous; I must remember how much I can take in future and not take more,' it is to be hoped that no great harm is done. But this is often not what happens at all. Bill comes home, falls over the milk bottles on the step and breaks them, kicks the cat, smacks the baby who has done nothing amiss, swears horribly at his wife, throws little John's infant-school drawing on the fire, strews some of his clothes on the landing and falls into bed with his boots on. In the morning his wife is upset. So Bill says pathetically, 'I can't call my soul my own. Can't a fellow have a couple of drinks now after doing a hard day's work?' 'A couple of drinks' is a self-justifying expression for perhaps ten drinks. Later, at work, Bill says something like, 'You know, my missus made no end of a fuss because I was a little merry last night.' 'Merry' sounds quite pleasant, gay, friendly; 'drunk', which is what Bill was, would be too self-condemnatory.

There was the experienced magistrate who said that if he was to believe the accused and the witnesses in all the cases concerning road accidents that he had heard, most collisions took place between two stationary cars each on the correct side of the road. The 'I' who is driving too fast is 'letting her rip'; the 'he' who is driving too fast is a 'road-hog'. There is a gruesome story, said to be true, of a man who was endangered by an accident on the river in a small boat. Another man gripped the edge of the boat to save himself from drowning; the speaker actually said later, 'So I had the *presence of mind* to strike him a hard blow over the knuckles, and he sank.' Some people would have called this something rather different.

This kind of whitewash language often amounts to downright lying; but it is not usually deliberate lying; it is born from our extreme unwillingness to attribute anything deplorable to ourselves. The most accurate and even pedantic professor of languages may find that his carefulness in the use of words disappears when he is explaining why he ought to have some special leave, or could not possibly have done the work he was supposed to do, or did not return that important book to the library!

Whitewash language is not confined to our personal lives; it is also much used by politicians and other persons in high authority. Then the actions of governments and parties, of police and armies, are whitewashed with language that sounds very pleasant. Sometimes this whitewash language is probably quite sincere; our capacity for believing what we wish to believe is such that self-deception is very easy; sometimes it must be cynical dishonesty; at least, it is difficult to see how some politicians can possibly believe the things they say, unless they hypnotize themselves or their senses are defective.

This is the kind of thing we are all familiar with:

'We make no claims that are not supported by the principles of truth and justice.'

We think so—perhaps.

'We shall defend the dignity and honour of our country to the last drop of our blood!'

We refuse to compromise, even to save the lives of many of our young men—and many of yours, too.

'Subversive elements have been suppressed and now we

can all go forward in unity to our glorious goal.'

The opposition has been killed, or imprisoned, or is missing, so the government can now do just as it pleases.

'Unproductive members of the community will no longer be allowed to share in the products of the community.'

At first sight this sounds fair, but it quite likely means, in politicians' language, that old and sick people have lost their ration cards.

'Un-American Activities.'

Anything that I, being an American with a particular set of rather inflexible opinions, disapprove of.

'Reactionary intrigues.'

Any relationships that I, being a Communist leader, disapprove of.

'Un-British.'

Anything that I, being British, think ought not to be done in Britain. An amusing story is told of a magistrate, who must have been rather pompous. A Dutch sailor was brought before him, charged with being drunk and disorderly. In the course of the trial evidence was given that the Dutch sailor had bitten someone's ear. The magistrate rebuked him with the words, 'It is very un-British to bite people.' Perhaps he thought that in Holland it was regarded as quite usual behaviour, but the captain of the ship gently intervened: 'It is very un-Dutch, too, my lord.'

'We hold a firm and serene conviction of the rightness of our cause.'

We have never stopped to think if we might possibly have made a mistake or if some concession or compromise might be wise and ethical.

'The Ruritanian Way of Life.'

The general structure of conventions, social order, pattern of activities, that I, being a Ruritanian, have become accustomed to in my particular class and group and generation.

'Our gallant soldiers have wiped out a few nests of in-surgents.'

The Army has killed, with overwhelming odds on its side, some people who disagree with the present Government and who were resorting to force to attack it.

'Our troops have retired to consolidate suitable positions further behind the lines.'

Our troops have had to retreat but hope they will have to retreat no further.

'Our troops have made a planned evacuation of Katzen-jammerburg and are moving as fast as possible southwards.'

The retreat has turned into a rout and the Army is running away as fast as it can.

'Katzenjammerburg has been liberated and has welcomed the democratic forces with enthusiasm.'

Katzenjammerburg is full of scattered loot, broken win-dows, outraged women and terror-stricken children. A few flags are hanging from a few windows.

'The enemy will not escape the just wrath of our people.'

We think we are succeeding in working up mob hysteria.

'The Minister is giving the matter his consideration.'

Nothing is being done.

'The Minister is giving the matter his active consideration.'

He might do something if you wrote another half-dozen nagging letters.

'We all passionately desire peace, but——'

We hope the other side will be blamed if war breaks out.

Yes; we all know the kind of language. At first it often sounds very reasonable; later it gets a laugh and is parodied; and a time comes when it makes people cynical and defeatist. There is in political life a great deal of sincere service and self-dedication, a great deal of idealism, and even a fair amount of practical sense. It is, however, a field of activity in which hypocrisy is particularly prevalent and words are often misused abominably. The habit of seriously examining the meaning of words is thus a protection to the public—from being swindled, from suicidal mob excitement, from allowing injustice to be done in its name, from those obsessive hatreds which in the end are as self-destructive as they are other-destructive.

The habit is also a protection for the politicians themselves. There is, after all, no intrinsic reason why trying to administer the large-scale affairs of a country—a job that somebody has to do—should involve the alternatives of headily total success and an undignified end in a prison yard or dangling from a lamp-post. . . .

XII. LANGUAGE OF QUARRELS

A FAILURE of communication may cause a quarrel. For example, two schoolgirls were in the cloakroom putting their outdoor clothes on. Joan's hat fell to the floor, and for some reason bounced several times. 'Goodness!' Evelyn exclaimed, 'the thing must be alive!' This remark, meant merely as a comment on the unusual liveliness of an inanimate object, was taken by Joan as implying that her hat was infested with lice, and she made a scene. We can even mishear a remark by failing to catch the tone of voice, and suppose ourselves insulted when we are merely being teased, or believe a word of praise to be sarcastic when it is sincere. Often one person hears something said about an absent friend, reports it in a slightly garbled form from genuine misunderstanding, and makes a great deal of mischief. A sincere and sensible woman said to another, in the course of conversation, 'I suppose I am rather strongly sexed.' This woman had great self-control and the observation was merely on the temperament she knew herself to have. Her hearer, not accustomed to this particular kind of frankness, went to a third party, and with the best intentions, in genuine anxiety for a younger person's happiness, told the third person she feared for the safety of the youngster, who was obviously about to do something very wrong and reckless! She was confusing a desire with the inability to handle it.

People who are trying to avoid quarrels are, therefore, wise to be careful with words and to try to ensure that they say what they mean and understand clearly what others mean. What happens to language when a real quarrel has already begun?

Truth, it has been said, is the first casualty in war; and it is the first casualty in any quarrel in which speech plays a part. For language in a quarrel rapidly degenerates, and that not merely in the sense that he who was at first *tiresome* may become *pig-headed*, then *a swine* and finally *a —— swine*. Our choice of invective and abuse will always depend mostly on our upbringing and habits; among some people a string of swear-words is no more than a recognized ornament to speech, and in other groups any use of such words is an unpardonable insult. A worse degeneration of language is that in a quarrel it gradually ceases to communicate. Language in a quarrel may be as useless and even as harmful as cancer cells are to the body; instead of fulfilling its proper function of communication, it erects new barriers.

The analysis of a typical quarrel-conversation may be unpleasant, but it may also be illuminating.

The quarrel arises because A has carelessly dropped some cigarette-ash on B's carpet while calling on B to discuss the date for a committee meeting.

B. Do you mind using the ash-tray, please?

(A reasonable request, couched in moderate terms, and not offensive provided that the tone of voice is friendly.)

A. Oh, sorry; didn't see it.

(A reasonable reply which is the end of the matter.) But suppose A is in a bad temper; then the conversation may go something like this.

A. Oh, all right, all right, don't fuss.

B. Here it is. Sorry, but it is my carpet, you know.

A. Never known such a fusspot as you!

(A, perhaps slightly conscious of being in the wrong in this small matter, and not wanting to feel in the wrong, tries to defend herself by an accusation against B. It might still not be the beginning of a quarrel, since *fusspot* is a good-humoured word, provided that the tone is not markedly hostile. But by now B too may be feeling a little annoyed.)

B. *Well, I'd rather be a fusspot than slovenly.*

A. *Oh, so I'm slovenly, am I?*

(B never said so; but A can argue that it was implied.)

B. *No, no. Don't be silly. Of course not.*

(The irritable tone is justifiable, but not wise, for A is now in a mood to take words in their most unfriendly sense, and no one likes to be called silly.)

A. *Oh, so now I am silly as well, am I?*

B. *No, but I shall begin to think you are if you take offence at every little thing.*

(At this point words still mean something and either A or B can prevent a serious quarrel; B by an affectionate or consoling remark instead of this rather self-righteous tone, A by a simple, brief apology, after which the subject should be changed. As A is the person most in the wrong, it is likely to be B who will have to take the initiative in making peace; such, rather unfairly, is life. This point, at which both persons are annoyed, is the danger point; and if the situation is not saved now the language will rapidly degenerate.)

A. *You think I'm bad-tempered! And do you know why I am bad-tempered?*

(One of those questions to which a tactful answer is almost impossible.)

Because I've had hardly any sleep for three nights, trying to work things out about this wretched committee! I'm working myself to death for the club and nobody appreciates me in the least! You've no idea what a burden I am carrying!

(Self-pitying language with obvious exaggerations.)

  B. Well, if the work is too much for you, why haven't you said so?

(A fair comment, but A does not want to be taken literally. B's question, on the face of it reasonable, sounds like further criticism.)

  A. And who says the work is too much for me? No one has ever complained that it wasn't properly done! (Unnecessary self-defence.) *And I couldn't ever say anything to you, however tired I was! No one can talk to you! You are too much wrapped up in yourself!*

(Accusation again as a means of defence. By now B too is losing patience at the repeated unfairness; and as soon as she loses patience she will become, not only rather self-righteous, but herself downright unfair.)

  B. Look here, there are plenty of people in the club who can talk to me; look at Ethel and Flora and how they tell me all their troubles! (Adding something inflammatory to what may be a true defence): *I'd like to see Flora telling you anything!*

  A. I don't care to make a cheap play for popularity with a bunch of moonstruck adolescents.

(Denigratory language.)

  B. You wouldn't make yourself popular with adolescents, either; if there's one thing they won't stand, it is whining insincerity.

(Oh dear! Now B too has reached a point of no return. That cannot be withdrawn except in total apology.)

  A. So now I know what you really think of me!

(No, she does not. What she now knows is that B, under some provocation, is also liable to say unkind, foolish and largely meaningless things.)

  B. Well, if the cap fits, wear it.

(A cliché that is no help; and for some reason such clichés generally sound smug.)

  A. You cat!

Language of Quarrels

B. *You silly woman!*

(Language has now degenerated into mere impolite expressions; communication has come to an end after decreasing for some time.)

A. *Oh, shut up! I'm sick of you!*

B. *Don't shout! I've come to the end of my patience with you!*

A. *That's the end of that! I'll send you my resignation in the morning!*

(And at this point either A goes out slamming the door, or A and B, having come to an end of meaningful speech, begin to scream, swear or weep, depending on their background and habits.)

I suppose no one old enough to read this book has escaped being, at some time, in one of these painful, ridiculous and almost always unnecessary situations. Not all quarrels can be avoided by ordinary, fallible and ordinarily selfish human beings; some people are extremely provocative, some differences of opinion extremely difficult to settle amicably; but well-intentioned people wish to avoid quarrels as far as possible. One check we can use is a certain perceptiveness about our own words; when we find that we are beginning to use words because they somehow give satisfaction in a mood of anger, and no longer because we genuinely wish to communicate something, we can try to pull ourselves up; we are about to plunge into a quarrel. Often the mere question, spoken in a mild and kindly tone, 'What is it we are really arguing about?' may be enough to turn language back from primitive noises into the channel of real communication. Soothing words are often as semantically empty as angry words; but they are more useful socially. Another check we can use is a perceptiveness about our neighbour's words; when we hear words slipping into this kind of meaninglessness, it is time to say something soothing and to try to restore communication. The last stage of a quarrel, when words have degenerated progressively away from communication, is a series of ugly animal howls; and these may easily turn into the opposite of human communication: blows.

A poignant and impressive example of the restoration of communication was seen some years ago at a conference in which Esperanto was the language used. Esperanto is available for use to anyone who finds it useful; but it is historically associated, for obvious reasons, with a general ideal of human understanding, brotherhood and the peaceful settlement of disputes, so that most active users of Esperanto are in some sense internationalists. At this conference some delegates from Western Europe and some delegates from Eastern Europe had a serious difference of opinion. As the argument developed, with strong feelings on both sides and a good deal of misinformation on both sides, words began to degenerate from instruments of communication to instruments of self-righteousness, then to the clichés of the propagandists, then to vulgar angry abuse and shouts. It seemed that in a few seconds the delegates would actually come to blows; the noise and facial expressions were already ugly. . . .

A plucky delegate who fortunately had a loud voice began to sing the international anthem of the Esperanto Movement. The shouting stopped just long enough for people to notice what they were doing . . . they realized that the whole point of learning Esperanto had been to understand one another, and that they were paradoxically quarrelling in it . . . words which had once seemed rather hackneyed were heard afresh with their full meaning . . . and the delegates, ashamed and calmed, began to join in the song. A few minutes later the discussion was resumed in a different spirit, using words to try to seek out the truth.

It might be said, then, that a serious, violent quarrel is temporarily *the death of language*; words lose their meaning, largely because the attempt at communication has ceased; in the last verbal stages of a quarrel we are generally not talking to the other person, but saying things that give satisfaction to ourselves. There is a less brutal kind of quarrel in which no settlement is possible until the meaning of words has been considered. Two people mean to communicate; the failure is not from temper but from real misunderstanding. This is very common in dispute between two people of different generations.

Definition is one of the keys to achievement. Here are some time-saving and misery-saving questions, for example:

'What is it exactly that you want?'

'Could you give me an idea of how much you expect of . . .?'

'Can we make an exchange, you do this and I do that?'

'Could we discuss a concrete example?'

'Can you tell me how?'

'If that isn't possible, what else can be done?'

'Would you consider settling for . . . ?'

'I am quite willing to do this. . . . Will that do for a start?'

'Shall we see how it works?'

'Can we agree first on . . . ?'

For instance, a mother tells her daughter she wants her to *behave properly*. The daughter is likely to turn round at this and say her mother is *fussy* and *old-fashioned*. This is the way to start a quarrel. However, while an unreasonable mother who wants to be a dictator will be angry if her daughter asks, 'What do you mean by *behaving properly*?' a mother who wants to educate her daughter will be willing to give some sort of example or definition. The daughter is then able to take part in a meaningful discussion and the two may reach some practical conclusions; but they will almost certainly have to include compromises on the way. For instance, Mother may then say that *proper behaviour* includes not wearing slacks, Daughter suggest that slacks are surely all right in the house and garden, Mother concede this but remain firm on wearing them for visiting other homes; Mother may say that proper behaviour forbids the use of lipstick, Daughter protest that all girls today wear it and that therefore it is embarrassingly unconventional not to do so, and Mother see her point, but suggest that too much lipstick looks jammy and that the colour should be suitable to the clothes and complexion of the wearer; Mother may say that it is not proper to walk along the street arm-in-arm with others so as to occupy the whole pavement and send other people into the gutter, and Daughter, on reflecting how inconvenient this behaviour is for others, may agree. And so two well-intentioned people, sitting by the fire and talking in a quiet manner, may learn much that is helpful, become better friends and practise the precious art of compromise instead of having a painful and useless quarrel. The attempt at *defining* proper behaviour instead of taking it for granted that Daughter knows what it means and wilfully disobeys, that Mother is nothing but a prim and proper old fuss-box to use such silly words, immediately leads to practical, meaningful discussion.

One of the tragedies of political life today is that so much discussion goes on without definition. Sometimes I find myself aching to hear of some statesman saying 'Gentlemen, would it not be a good idea to decide what we are talking about?' Nearly all political speeches of a controversial nature have in them some element of quarrel-language, of meaningless language functioning not as communication, but as self-applause or as abuse of the other side. Real wants are disguised in clouds of language suggestive of shining virtue and disinterestedness; sometimes the man in the street (who is also likely to become the man in the hole in the street when bombs begin to fall) feels that it might be better if the politi-

Language of Quarrels

cians said what they wanted—though of course this would not in itself solve the very complex problems of present-day politics. Co-operation between groups of people whose immediate interests differ is never going to be easy; words will not in themselves abolish selfishness or produce forethought; but co-operation and reasonableness are aided whenever human beings show determination to use words as instruments of communication, and firmly reject the degenerate use of words.

XIII. LYING TO OURSELVES

THERE are very few people who do not now and then tell a deliberate lie. What might be called a full, deliberate lie is not merely the careless use of words, but a statement known to be objectively untrue. 'It was Peter who stole the buns!' says Jim, who stole them himself. 'I have not seen Anne for six weeks!' says Philip, who has been meeting her regularly behind the barn. 'This is my last territorial claim in Europe!' said Hitler, shortly before making a further claim.

If, however, we consider the number of things said by the average person every day, the number of full, deliberate lies is a small percentage of our whole communication; much social life is based on the assumption that most people tell the truth most of the time, at least in the sense of not making deliberate total mis-statements. Modern commerce, for instance, has to be based on a large measure of mutual trust. So have personal relations; so has the appointment of people to jobs; so, indeed, has ordinary conversation. We recognize the difference between the person who occasionally, under some kind of pressure, tells a lie, and the person whose words are never to be trusted, the 'pathological liar'. Most of us regard direct lies as 'wrong' and would differ only in assessing those situations in which some would say a lie is excusable (someone whose business it clearly is not asks me an impertinent question about my private life) or even a positive duty (a homicidal maniac runs into the room with a knife in his hand and asks me where my mother is) or accepted as a social convention ('Mrs. Warwick is not at home').

To me one of the great evils of a totalitarian or even an over-conventional society is that it tends to force well-meaning but unheroic people to tell more lies than they otherwise would, from fear. Where there is constant fear of, and expectation of, unjust and unreasonable treatment, most people will get into the habit of lying; it is a needful part of self-protection; and the habit may soon extend beyond what is necessary. Even in so unimportant a tyranny as a highly authoritarian and punishment-ridden school or family this mechanism may be seen at work.

However, most people would agree that telling deliberate lies is wrong, except perhaps in certain special situations where more harm will be done by telling the truth. Even the most truthful people probably tell a good many more lies that might be regarded as *semantic lies*; their use of words contains some measure of falsehood, more or less deliberate.

'Do you think it is right to rag Mr. Dickenson? Ink-pellets flying, a white mouse in his desk, silly sentences in your exercises—do you realize how badly you are behaving?'

'Oh,' the schoolboy replies, 'Mr. Dickenson doesn't mind; he is always a good sport.'

To this boy 'a good sport' is someone who will meekly put up with stupid insults and time-wasting; this praise is an excuse for continuing to treat the master in a very *un*sporting fashion.

'I can't see you now; I am too busy.' I say to one of my pupils. This may be true; but it is more likely that I do not want to take the trouble to replan my replannable work so that I can see her.

'I don't think that bathing costume is decent, showing all

Lying to Ourselves

that much of herself!' says Mrs. Lumpe indignantly; what she really means is, 'I wish she would not show her lovely figure, because I know I should look like a piece of pink pork in a costume like that.' And so on.

The average human being tells a direct lie relatively rarely and is conscious of this as wrong. He or she tells semantic lies more often, probably does not regard them as wrong and is often barely conscious of their insincerity. I should say that all of us *lie to ourselves*, in part, almost as a continuous process. Not all of this is verbal; we do not think continuously in words; but only when we put our thoughts into words can we make any examination of their truthfulness. The process of becoming conscious is a difficult one; many people do not even wish to be conscious; and modern psychology tells us that a large part of what goes on in our minds is normally inaccessible.

The reactions of many people to modern psychological theory, especially the theories of Sigmund Freud, provide interesting and pathetic examples of our taste for lying to ourselves. Freud laid great stress on the importance of our sexual desires and experiences and curiosities in shaping our lives. To someone who is trying to be honest, such theories are, like any other theories, something to be examined, investigated, accepted or rejected, or—as is usually the best reaction to most theories—partly accepted as containing some useful truths or working hypotheses, but not accepted unconditionally as a new revelation, in that all scientific 'truth' is provisional and may be outdated by further research. Many people, however, found it distasteful to suppose that their sexual feelings played as great a part in their lives as Freud said. Not many such people told themselves, 'I do not want to think about such theories; they embarrass me and make me feel I am just an animal, not dignified. I feel they are not pleasant ideas, and it will make me unhappy to think about

K   133

them, so I will not think about them; the theories I have
about life seem to work all right for me and I do not need
new ideas.'

While this is perhaps rather an ostrich-like attitude, it
would be fundamentally honest; and there may indeed be
good sense, for a nervous or timid person, in refusing to
think about subjects that cause anxiety. But the people who
refused to pay any attention to Freud's startling theories often
commended themselves for their 'virtue' in finding them
distasteful; this was really an excuse made to themselves for
not having the courage to face what they found unpalatable.

'He must have been a dirty old man to have had such filthy
ideas. I am a good woman and I am not going to soil my
mind with such nastiness. The world is going to the dogs;
when I was a girl no one would even have dared to say such
things; but I shall keep my mind pure, even if everyone else
swallows all this modern wickedness.'

The woman who says this is almost certainly *not* deliberately lying. She is to some extent lying semantically—
scientific research described scientifically may err even
wildly, but it cannot be 'dirty'; and she is obviously using
a 'good woman' and 'pure' in an extremely limited and
inadequate sense; but she is not doing this consciously.
What she is doing is *lying to herself*; and this we all do every
day.

I tell myself I am *honest*; and I sincerely believe, when I say
this, that I am: I never steal, I do not cheat the Customs or
the Income Tax; I pay my debts promptly; I have never
sold anything under false pretences . . . and then I stop to
think a little harder. I am lying to myself; I am not honest.
Yesterday I was five minutes late for my work, for which
I am being paid on the assumption that it begins at a given
time. This morning I took rather more than my fair share of
butter at breakfast. And I said last night that I had no time

134

to deal with a problem and would see to it tomorrow, when the truth was that I badly wanted to write some private letters. . . . Well then, I may be a human being trying hard, but I cannot call myself *honest*.

John does not care for cultural activities—music, painting, reading, serious discussions. He is entirely at liberty not to; there are plenty of other ways of enjoying life and of being useful. But does he tell himself: 'I haven't much brains and I am mentally rather lazy, so I am not intending to bother with the arts'? No! He is far more apt to say, 'I am a real man, I am not a sissy; I am not one of those degenerate egg-heads, those drawing-room intellectuals.'

The people I know with the most insatiable appetite for culture happen to include an ex-guerilla fighter and freedom-radio broadcaster, a professional explorer and a former bomber pilot; but the legend that cultured people are soft and unmanly is a very useful excuse for the mentally lazy and the insensitive.

Katherine is lacking in mental adventurousness, is afraid of new ideas and new activities, and is afflicted with the kind of intolerance that arises from timidity. On her lips we constantly hear such words as *wholesome, healthy, normal, nice, decent, the done thing, not quite the thing, respectable*. She disguises her fears as virtues and learns to be proud of her limitations. On the other hand, Roger, with no sense of responsibility, who goes through life causing unhappiness to others and leaving others to clear up his messes is quite likely to praise himself as *adventurous, unconventional, enterprising, daring, uninhibited* and so forth; and, like Katherine, he does not stop to think if a few careful definitions might not lead him to some uncomfortable opinions about life and the self. We do not usually lie to ourselves wilfully; but we all do it unintentionally. People who think they are in love but whose 'love' is really shallow and immature sometimes deceive on purpose; but more often they deceive themselves first. How easily we can convince ourselves that our anger is *righteous* anger! and how easily we can convince ourselves that we are *broken-hearted* when we are merely angry and disappointed! How easily we can believe that *we never had a chance* when what has really prevented our success is that we never took one! While there are certainly some people who are deliberately dishonest, insincere, hypocritical, the vast majority of us are probably the self-deceived, and most of the time deceive others only as a by-product.

What are the reasons for this? One reason is certainly the desire of a healthy person to think fairly well of himself; and the unhealthy mind that is determined to think ill of itself is just as self-deceiving with the disadvantage that it is miserable too. This might be called the moral reason: we have a weakness of pride, a rather pathetic little vanity of wanting to have good motives for all we do; and we may add to this, often, a desire that if we cannot be good we may at least live rather dramatically. I have myself probably deceived myself more in the process of trying to think myself interesting than in trying to think myself good!

Then there is what might be called an intellectual reason: the simple and inevitable fact that none of us are sufficiently intelligent to understand even ourselves completely, let alone other people or the general meaning of human life. Very little can be done about this. The great Greek exhortation 'Know Thyself' is excellent advice, is the foundation of psychology and the beginning of charity; but it is impossible ever to obey it adequately.

Third, there is what might be called the verbal reason. There are enough words for all the kinds of grass in the world, all the cloud formations, all the possible chemical compounds. . There are not, and I do not see how there can ever be, enough words to differentiate human emotions and experiences. A word like *love, faith, mercy, justice, pride, anger, pity, wisdom, glory,* or *fear* has to carry a load of assorted meanings that makes it well-nigh impossible for any two people, at a given moment, to understand it in precisely the same sense. And it is in the realm of emotions, human relations and ethics that we are most apt to fall into self-deception. Only a fool or a deliberate liar says, 'There are six eggs in the basin!' when he can see that there are four pears in it; but in the course of history millions of decent kindly men must have said to millions of women, 'I love you!' and brought them immeasurable unhappiness because the words were understood in two different senses by speaker and hearer; and millions of parents must have said, 'It is all for your own good!' and so appeared to be callous hypocrites, when in fact the total situation was far more complex than anyone could provide words to explain.

It seems to me, then, that it is very important to try to use words honestly and to think about what words mean; and that a certain reverent care for meaning will tend to improve human relationships on both a small and a large scale; but also that full communication is impossible and that, because of human limitations, we must to some extent resign ourselves to life being a tissue of lies, not deliberate lies, but a mixture of semantic and psychological confusion.

What is the inference from that last fact?

Charity. The study of meaning may at first give us a sense that we are very clever, with a lawyer-like subtlety; we enjoy our new perceptions and we think for a time that we have the key to truth. Then, as we realize how much all communication is limited, even within our own minds, we come to the painful knowledge that at best we know very little. The inference from that need not be any kind of despair; it can be a generous, sympathetic tolerance, arising from the awareness that every human being is trapped in the same ignorance, the same inadequacy. Truth, it might be said, is the inspirer and the instrument of justice; but the awareness of our own fallibility is the foundation of mercy.

PART III

Literary Semantics

XIV. RHETORIC

Most of this book is devoted to what might be called the semantics of everyday life; and if we are thinking about the meaning of words we can never go far away from human beings, human problems and human relationships, since the purpose of words is to communicate and we do not communicate with the empty air. Moreover, semantics would be a mere pedantic exercise if human relationships were not involved, and on the contrary it is a study of great importance to human sincerity and happiness. However, the last two chapters will deal superficially with the meaning of words as used in poetry and rhetoric; in the verbal arts, which are in one sense operating at one remove from 'real life' and in another sense, being created by human beings, are still as much a part of real life as eggs and bacon.

Today *rhetoric* is very nearly a dirty word. *Rhetorical language* is almost a synonym for exaggerated and insincere language. It is not fashionable to like 'purple patches', and today much writing that was once regarded as beautiful is thought of as high-flown, even comical. Have we gone too far now in the direction of distrusting rhetoric? and are we not perhaps falling into a new sort of cliché, the 'dirty-word' use of *rhetorical* as a term dismissing all emotional, all metaphorical. all picturesque language as insincere? I have tried to point out that there is a great difference between sentiment and sentimentality, that emotion is a necessary and indeed a desirable part of human life; a distinction should also be made between legitimate and illegitimate rhetoric.

If we remember that the purpose of language is communication, we may be able to arrive at some concept of the function of rhetoric. Rhetorical language is not trying to communicate in the same manner; but it may still be communicating; and the best rhetorical language may be communicating more intensely, more, so far as we can judge, truthfully, than any literal, objective statements.

'The toast is on fire!' I exclaim. Everyone who understands the language knows what I mean. The bread I was roasting is blackening and flaming. There is no doubt. This may possibly be a lie, but it cannot be an ambiguous statement.

Another day I say something rhetorical instead of literal: 'I am on fire with love!' As a joke, someone may reply, 'Fetch a bucket of water!' However, no one thinks for one second that I mean that I am blackening and flaming. This hackneyed metaphor is an attempt at conveying a particular kind of rather obsessive emotion which is in part a physical experience.

Rhetoric is often needed, because language is not adequate for expressing emotion. Metaphor, simile, association, personification, analogy can indeed mislead when used dishonestly, but they can also be used honestly in an attempt to communicate. Indeed, one of the criteria of good rhetoric is that it should be sincere; inflated rhetoric is essentially insincere. The soggy pseudo-rhetoric found in some political speeches and some sermons, in the worst kind of family quarrels ('I work my fingers to the bone for you . . .') and in some of the love scenes of very poor plays and films is an imitation of the rhetoric generated by real emotions. Bad over-flowery writing, too, is an imitation of great rhetorical writing; and some rhetorical writers tend to parody themselves in their less creative moments; for example, D. H.

Lawrence can at times convey impressions of intense and complicated emotion with electric vitality; but he can also sometimes imitate himself and become inflated.

It is not 'unnatural' to use figurative language. I have heard a barely literate but fundamentally sensitive man say, gazing with awe at a tiger in a cage, 'Eee, but its fur looks like hot coals behind bars!' and a quite unliterary woman suddenly refer with delight to the 'meringues on the hawthorn trees' (the masses of blossom). Some time ago I teased a very sincere and unaffected woman whose husband, though a most kind and humane man, had a rather formidable appearance: 'I don't wonder you collect stones; I suppose you were looking for a lump of granite when you found your husband?' 'No,' she replied at once, 'you forgot that I collect pieces of pure crystal too.' Strong emotions often bring surprisingly rhetorical language out of people with no literary pretensions; the struggle to say something during courtship that is adequate to express feelings for which no human language can have words often produces metaphors and hyperboles; very angry people also often come out with rhetorical expressions; and so do people in great distress. Proverbs, which are not literary but folk art, bear witness to the naturalness of such language: 'There's never smoke without fire', 'All that glitters is not gold', 'The cat would eat fish and not wet her feet' are not useful contributions to knowledge if we take them literally.

Affected and tiresome rhetoric occurs in conjunction with sentimentality or in the imitation of genuine rhetorical speech. Wordsworth explains this admirably in an appendix to the Preface to the *Lyrical Ballads*:

'The earliest poets of all nations generally wrote from passion excited by real events; they wrote naturally, and as men: feeling powerfully as they did, their language was daring, and figurative. In succeeding times, Poets, and Men ambitious of the fame of Poets, perceiving the influence of such language, and desirous of producing the same effect without being animated by the same passion, set themselves to a mechanical adoption of these figures of speech, and made use of them, sometimes with propriety, but much more frequently applied them to feelings and thoughts with which they had no natural connection whatsoever. A language was thus insensibly produced, differing materially from the real language of men in *any situation*. The Reader or Hearer of this distorted language found himself in a perturbed and unusual state of mind: when affected by the genuine language of passion he had been in a perturbed and unusual state of mind also: in both cases he was willing that his common judgment and understanding should be laid asleep, and he had no instinctive and infallible perception of the true to make him reject the false; the one served as a passport for the other. The emotion was in both cases delightful, and no wonder if he confounded the one with the other, and believed them both to be produced by the same, or similar causes.'

There are occasions when it is perfectly permissible for a politician to say something like 'a crime which has shocked the conscience of every Christian community in Europe'. What kind of crime? Perhaps Hitler's persecutions of the Christian Churches; or the action of Christian priests who swear oaths of allegiance to dictator régimes; or the fact that some priests had been using the threat of excommunication to influence voting in an election; something large, clearly wrong or at least violently controversial; comprehensible to everyone and of general importance. When F. E. Smith said that the Welsh Disestablishment Bill—something essentially local, highly technical and not a black-and-white moral question, was 'a Bill which has shocked the conscience of every Christian community in Europe', G. K. Chesterton wrote his famous 'Chuck it, Smith!' satirical poem, pointing out that the language was ridiculously immoderate in relation to the circumstances:

> 'In the mountain hamlets clothing
> Peaks beyond Caucasian pales,
> Where Establishment means nothing
> And they never heard of Wales,
> Do they read it all in Hansard
> With a crib to read it with—
> "Welsh Tithes: Dr. Clifford Answered."
> Really, Smith?'

Chesterton himself was one of the most rhetorical writers imaginable; his objection was not to F. E. Smith's rhetoric but to its disproportion to the subject, in other words, its sentimentality.

There is inevitably something comic in an egg-bald man's plea that his ungrateful children will bring down his grey hairs in sorrow to the grave, or a fat woman's declaration that she is wasting away for love, though both expressions might be meaningful and touching in another context. When someone says 'I wish I was dead!' he very seldom means it, though on rare occasions someone does say this with full meaning and it is then a very terrible thing to hear. Similarly 'I've got no one but you in all the world!' is very rarely true . . . but just occasionally it may be.

The functions of rhetoric seem to me to be as follows:

1. To communicate emotion and other experiences that cannot be communicated by means of factual, literal language.

2. To induce emotion, perhaps emotion leading to action, in other people.

3. To adorn speech and writing.

We must accept the communication of emotion as a reasonable human desire; and if we also accept, as I do, that our greatest satisfactions are found in our emotional lives, it is very important for our happiness and evolution that we should talk about emotions. Legitimate rhetoric in this field, then, seeks really to communicate emotion. It is illegitimate when it falls into *sentimentality*, which has already been defined. Emotion may be communicated by hyperbole:

> Were you the earth, dear love, and I the skies,
> My love should shine on you like to the sun,
> And look upon you with ten thousand eyes,
> Till heav'n waxed blind and till the world were dun.
> JOSHUA SYLVESTER, 1563–1618 (from a sonnet)

and it may be said that the hyperbole is meant to convince us of the violence of the emotion;

by metaphor:

> A single violet transplant,
> The strength, the colour, and the size,
> (All which before was poor and scant)
> Redoubles still, and multiplies.
> When love with one another so
> Interinanimates two souls,
> That abler soul, which thence doth flow,
> Defects of loneliness controls.
> JOHN DONNE, 1573–1631: *The Ecstasy*

where an analogy is used to try to convey to us a psychological experience for which we have no adequate vocabulary:

by drastic, adventurous and unexpected language:

> I am soft sift
> In an hourglass—at the wall
> Fast, but mined with a motion, a drift,
> And it crowds and combs to the fall;
> GERARD MANLEY HOPKINS, 1844–1889:
> *The Wreck of the Deutschland*

where the function of language is not only to convey emotion by analogy, but also, as it were, to wake us up, to startle us into noticing by some unusual stimulus.

People with little understanding of the use of poetry often complain that a poem is 'difficult'. I have heard it brought more than once as a serious complaint against a poem: 'You have to read it several times before you understand it'! There is an obscurity which is caused by careless writing and insufficient concern for communication; but most 'difficult' poetry is 'difficult' precisely because the poet is trying to do something very difficult indeed, to convey a complicated and delicate experience to other people. If an adequate vocabulary for emotion and the inner life existed, there might be no 'difficulty' poetry. As it is, the remarkable thing is that some poetry and rhetorical prose do seem to come fairly near to conveying a satisfactory impression of emotional phenomena.

It is very difficult to assess the sincerity of an emotional statement; most of us do so by methods which we could not ourselves fully explain, which are often more intuitive than intellectual; they depend very much on that indefinable quality we often call the *tone* of a speech, poem, personal conversation and so on. One of the biggest difficulties here is that what is a mark of insincerity in one person may be perfectly authentic in another. For example, in general it is more likely that rhetorical language which is an imitation of someone else's language will be insincere, than that something original will be; the passage from Wordsworth quoted above explains this admirably; but, on the other hand, people of relatively little verbal ingenuity are naturally apt to turn to expressions they have previously heard to express what they themselves cannot find words for; it is natural to quote works with which we are familiar, such as the Bible; and the expressions of strong and usual human emotions may tend to coincide without imitation being involved. For example, when some years ago my father died, and my mother said to me (an only child), 'Now we have only got each other!' this might well have sounded to an outsider like something sentimental, imitative and out of a book; but since such a thing has often been in some sense *true* it will also be often *said*; and my mother is an exceptionally sincere person. It was the same person who, wishing to appeal to a Government department a little later for some concession, looked up in the process of wording a letter to say, 'Can I say, My husband has recently died in tragic circumstances? No, I don't suppose I can; if in the middle of a world war he died a natural and painless death, I have no business to use the word *tragic*, have I?' This struck me at the time as something like heroic semantic honesty.

Moreover, some people genuinely feel much more strongly than others about various things. There are people who do not ever 'fall in love' and who, if they marry, marry for companionship or convenience; there are people who are surprisingly philosophical about misfortune; there are people who hardly react at all to slanders and insults; and so on. To people of naturally unemotional temperaments many expressions of strong emotion may well sound like a great fuss over nothing; the most genuine, passionate and urgent real emotions may sound like sentimentality. In England, a country in which the violent expression of emotion tends to be disapproved of, with an excellent effect on our formal manners and political stability and probably often a bad effect on the psychological health of individuals (and possibly one factor in the high proportion of gastric ulcers and chronic catarrh!), we are very apt to suspect insincerity in the more emotional expressive and dramatic manner of a Slav or Southern European. I have certainly not had this suspicion confirmed by my intimate knowledge of many such people; and we should remember that many foreigners suspect us of being much more hypocritical than the average English person really is, because of our tradition of restrained expression. My own view is that we should be slow to suspect real insincerity, and should judge sincerity by the relation of people's deeds to their words, rather than by the nature of the words themselves.

If a woman says, 'My religion is everything to me; I could not breathe without it!' she may or may not be sincere; but if she then puts a button in the collection and spreads stories about the minister that are known to be untrue, she must be insincere. If a man says to a woman, 'I love you; I adore you; I want to protect you against all the rough ways of the world and look after you as my treasure!' he may be absolutely sincere; but if he then humiliates the woman in front of others and stands wondering what to do when another man insults her, he must be insincere. Even then we must remember that *insincerity* is by no means always the same as *deliberate deceit*, that most of us lie to ourselves before we lie to others. Being honest is difficult, even strenuous, not only morally but intellectually.

What about the use of rhetorical methods to induce emotion in other people? Here words are used with the hope that their forcefulness or unusual quality will startle:

'Are you dogs, or worms, or little bits of slime, or grown men?'

(A rhetorical question assuming that the hearers will wish to reply, 'Grown men!')

'I do not have a soul!' said the priest from the pulpit, and shocked his orthodox hearers. 'I have a body'—and shocked them more. 'I *am* a soul.'

(Rhetorical use of an ambiguity in the word *have* to remind his congregation that to a Christian the soul is more important than the body and the body merely a vehicle or vessel.)

Or words may be used in the hope that the rich structure

of association around them will stimulate the emotions of the hearers.

'I implore you to think again before you pass this law. Do not think only of your own prestige, of the prestige of this parliament. Think also of bewildered women and of the children who may be made homeless by an administrative formula. I have explained how injustice might be done; think of your own wives; how would you feel if they were to suffer the humiliation this law might bring them? Think of your own children; think of the horror that would sicken you if you knew your own children were to be made homeless! Those innocent children you love, with their bright trusting eyes and the light on their hair. . . .'

It may be supposed that earlier in the speech the speaker's appeal was objective, explanatory and factual; but now he is trying to arouse emotion, by appealing to personal experience and so make things more real. Is this legitimate? I think it depends entirely on the context and motive. There is honest rhetoric, which aims at skilfully applying psychological-verbal techniques in order to arouse emotions in others, without deliberate deceit and for a good motive; and there is dishonest rhetoric, which uses the same techniques deceitfully, for a discreditable reason . . . and cold-bloodedly. A great and good orator is sincere; it is from his own emotions that he produces the words with which he can arouse emotion in others. A demagogue uses words skilfully, but this is the use of a formula, a deliberate, cunning working upon other people's feeling.

If we read the wartime speeches of Sir Winston Churchill, or the most famous speeches of Edmund Burke or of John Bright, we may find that we disagree with many of the opinions expressed; but we do not, I think, find outselves muttering 'Cant!' The opinions are such as we feel a rational and well-meaning person might hold; the rhetorical devices make the expression of them more forceful. The brief and very impressive Gettysburg Oration of Abraham Lincoln is a superb piece of rhetoric; but it rings true; Lincoln had a reputation for sincerity that few politicians have enjoyed before or since. The emotion itself seems to be generating the rhetoric that moves us.

Was Hitler sincere? Perhaps he deceived himself before he deceived his people and wrecked a world; but some of his lies were so obvious, and he himself admitted so openly to the deliberate technique of 'the big enough lie', that we may safely assume at least some insincerity; was his rhetoric good in the aesthetic sense? So far as I have been able to find out, it seems not. His power over an audience seems to have depended relatively little on eloquent words, but to have been a matter of endless reiteration and a rather hysterical manner —hysteria is notoriously very catching.

It is, of course, not possible to say that every orator of whose principles or aims we do not approve is insincere; this is merely making *insincere* another 'dirty word'. For example, today some political orators, especially in the Middle East, try to propagate an exaggerated nationalism that is quite unsuitable to their epoch and will not, in the long run, be the most beneficial attitude for their peoples to take; but most of these fanatical nationalists are probably sincere. *Insincere* rhetoric occurs only when orators *try to induce in other people emotions that they do not themselves feel, largely by pretending to feel them.* Fortunately, emotion is so much the driving power of art that the best orators artistically may generally be expected to be sincere, however wrong-headed they may seem.

Related to this is the fact that much very bad public speaking includes not only poor verbal expression, but actual muddle-headedness in thought. It is very difficult to arouse emotions in other people unless we both feel them ourselves, and are able to justify them to ourselves.

Rhetoric

The strictly *moral* criterion that we may at times apply to rhetoric is a good deal more limiting than the artistic criterion of sincerity; when we are considering whether it is right to make a given speech, we must also consider whether the emotions the orator wishes to arouse are desirable and whether the action to which these emotions may lead is a good action. Few people would object to a passionate, rhetorical speech appealing to an assembly to contribute money to aid refugee children; indeed, even if the speaker was deliberately working his emotion up a little artificially, the cause is so good that most of us would not be unduly anxious about the details of the method. But a man might be absolutely sincere in his passionate, fanatical hatred of, say, the country's president; if he used his passionate oratory to induce a mob to burn down the president's house and trample the president to death, very few people could feel that his sincerity was a justification for his behaviour. These, however, are questions of ethics, not of semantics.

Lastly, rhetoric may be used simply to adorn speech and writing. Figures of speech may not be necessary to clarify, or to stimulate emotion, but may still be used for the sheer pleasure they give. I sometimes give a humorous lecture in English or Esperanto on some completely unimportant subject such as 'My Well-Planned Kitchen' (the title itself is rhetorical, the figure of speech used being irony!); 'His Mewing Excellency—From the Life of a Siamese Cat'; or some journey I have made, with emphasis on the funny side. These talks, if they were simply straightforward accounts of the everyday and valueless subjects, would be of no interest at all; the whole point of a humorous lecture is *the way the stories are told*. Irony, comical exaggeration, climaxes, sudden anti-climaxes, surprises of every kind, puns, odd comparisons and so on, ludicrous understatements, unexpected epithets, are what make a talk of this kind; the pleasure of the listener is not in the valueless subject-matter, but in the comical language. I have at times been restrained only by sympathy and courtesy from yawning at what might be expected to be a very affecting story of some dramatic, tragic personal experience; I remember once laughing until tears ran from my eyes when a famous orator was doing nothing but describe a nervous old lady eating her meal in a hotel. I once heard someone describe the death of a sow so skilfully that it was impossible not to feel grief. I have heard a professional lecturer give an account of a minor car accident in such a way that it was a remarkable comedy-drama.

Delight in language, as it were for its own sake, is, then, an aspect of rhetoric. This is a direct unadorned statement:

'Percy had a very much larger appetite than the average man.'

Here is what is essentially the same statement, made into a piece of frivolous rhetoric:

'To say that Percy was fond of eating would be rather like saying that a lighted match is fond of petrol. Nothing edible could be placed within his reach without being instantly consumed. To him four pork chops with fried potatoes were a snack to stay his stomach between meals; and a full-grown boiling fowl was not enough for two persons. He wished that oranges grew as large as footballs, and found that a melon merely stimulated his appetite without satisfying it. A full-size family fruit cake was a fortress to be sacked and razed to the ground; and when gooseberry or apple pie was on the table, his *pie*ty was exemplary. When the housing problem was at its worst, there was always room inside Percy; when the buses were crowded, Percy always had room for a few more inside. To offer him a sweet was like dropping a stone into a well; the stone disappears but the well still gapes. Percy could not see a pretty girl without thinking that the meat off her would be tasty with apple sauce; to him the clouds were meringues and the copse in the valley was a salad bowl; the sand made him think of ginger cake and the rocks of parkin; the snow seemed to him like the icing on a global cake and we suspected that he regarded the sun itself as a cosmic cooking stove. The only abstraction he could appreciate was Time, since that is said to devour all things, and this at once waked some fellow-feeling in Percy, the respect of a man for a competent senior colleague.'

This is not the language of statement; its exaggerations are so obvious as to be free from danger, its details are really repetitions not contributions to our knowledge. It is the language of fun. Any study of the meaning of words which never takes into account that language is sometimes just fun, or just emotional outlet, is inadequate.

An obvious example of this is that when people swear they are very, very rarely conscious of any relationship between the swear-word and its apparent meaning. Without going into the details of the more grossly offensive language, we can consider such expressions as this—which an uncle of mine claims really to have heard, 'So I told 'im to sit down for five minutes, for 'e was as white as a bloody sheet!' Most people who allow themselves to swear at all have almost certainly, at some time, consigned something or someone to 'hell' when in fact their feelings towards that thing or person were usually friendly. A foolish and vulgar habit; but perhaps not as bad a habit as sentimentality, if we are to measure our behaviour by its consequences.

As a Hungarian friend of mine once put it, a good deal of what we say is giving our mouth an airing, not communication. This is, indeed, probably a necessary function of language; we all know how suffering is relieved by talking the trouble out, and some psychologists today positively encourage their patients to use very violent, emotional language in order to get rid of the harmful emotional tensions that have caused the illness. Trouble arises from the loosely emotional use of language, or from language used in fun, only when the ornamental aspect of language is mistaken for communicative language. If I say to someone, 'Really, you are an idiot; look, you have punctuated that sentence so that it makes no sense!' and she takes 'idiot' as my giving my mouth an airing, no great harm is done; but if she receives the impression that I genuinely regard her as mentally defective, she may become quite unable to work for me. So usually I prefer, when merely being playfully abusive, to use some term such as 'silly sausage', which, since my pupil is never in any doubt that she is not a sausage, cannot be harmfully misunderstood. It would be a pity to renounce the fun, the gaiety, the ornamental quality, of figures of speech, the delight of rhetoric and its comfort, from a puritanical, Platonic feeling that such language was telling lies. What matters is that we should try to say what we mean in all those contexts in which it matters to human happiness that we should fully mean what we say.

XV. METAPHOR AND ASSOCIATION

METAPHOR is probably the most important and frequent figure of speech in poetry and in rhetorical prose.

> But true love is a durable fire
> In the mind ever burning. . . .
> ANONYMOUS (sixteenth century)

> We seek to know the moving of each sphere
> And the strange cause of th'ebbs and floods of Nile
> But of that clock within our breasts we bear
> The subtle motion we forget the while.
> <div align="right">SIR JOHN DAVIES (1569–1626): <i>Nosce Teipsum</i></div>

> My hasting days fly on with full career,
> But my late spring no bud or blossom shew'th.
> JOHN MILTON (1608–1674)

> He gave us this eternal spring
> Which here enamels everything;
> ANDREW MARVELL (1621–1678):
Song of the Emigrants in Bermuda

> How the Chimney-sweeper's cry
> Every black'ning Church appalls;

And the hapless Soldier's sigh
Runs in blood down Palace walls.
WILLIAM BLAKE (1757–1827)

This Sea that bares her bosom to the moon. . . .
WILLIAM WORDSWORTH (1770–1850)

I fall upon the thorns of life! I bleed!
P. B. SHELLEY (1792–1822): *Ode to the West Wind*

and in my breast
Spring wakens too, and my regret
Becomes an April violet,
And buds and blossoms like the rest.
ALFRED TENNYSON (1809–1892): *In Memoriam*

In paradise, the fruits were ripe, the first minute,
and in heaven it is alwaies Autumne, his mercies are
ever in their maturity.
JOHN DONNE (1573–1631): from a sermon

Who are you, that you should fret and rage, and bite
the chains of Nature? Nothing worse happens to
you than does to all Nations who have extensive
Empire; and it happens in all the forms into
which Empire can be thrown. In large bodies, the
circulation of power must be less vigorous at the
extremities.
EDMUND BURKE (1729–1797): from his speech
on conciliation with America

Such figures of speech as simile and personification have a
very similar purpose and effect. For the purposes of this
chapter they can generally be considered as a part of *meta-*
M   157

phorical language, which differs so much from *literal language* that its meaning cannot be regarded as *meaning* in the same sense.

Metaphor is an attempt at communicating something, usually but not always something emotional, which literal language cannot communicate, or which metaphorical language will communicate more vividly and intensely. It may seem to be merely ornamental; but in good writing these 'ornaments' generally add something to intensity, if not to meaning.

One thing metaphor is not; it is not *unnatural*. We are often tempted to talk as if it were; but metaphor is a part of everyday speech, so much so that we often use metaphors without even realizing that we are doing so. It is to be found in the very history of language: *zest*, for example, originally meant *lemon peel* used for flavouring; zest is the quality of mind and manner that gives life a piquant, pleasant 'flavour'; *stupid* comes from a word meaning *stunned*; we speak of moral *obliquity* just as we speak colloquially of someone who is *not straight*; a *flagrant* offence is philologically a *blazing* one. The most scrupulous avoider of evocative or rhetorical language cannot carry on a conversation without sometimes using a word in which a dead metaphor lies hidden; and everyday slang is full of metaphors. We give somebody beans, we are in the soup, we tell someone to go and boil his head, we are like a dog with two tails, our tiresome children have sent us up the wall, we lose our heads, we show a leg, we wash our hands of the matter, we get something off our chest, or we listen with half an ear. We are not intentionally using figurative language when we use such expressions, highly figurative though they are; we are using expressions that we have long taken for granted.

Metaphor thus seems to be an innate and entirely natural aspect of the language, not only of artists but of non-artistic, even banal, human beings. It is closely related to analogy; a metaphor when it is original is an attempt to explain something by means of something else. A savage who had never seen an aeroplane might be given some notion of the meaning of the word by saying, 'It is a very large bird, as large as a hut, but it is not alive; it is the image of a bird made from metal, and it can fly for many hours. Men and women can sit in the stomach of the bird and so make journeys.' Scientifically speaking, this is most inaccurate, but it is an analogy which would mean something to the savage and would enable him to recognize an aeroplane when he saw one. Anyone who knows what cancer is understands such an expression as: 'Don't let yourself become envious, for envy is a sort of *cancer of the soul*.' If I say that in a crisis of my life some friend has been a *rock*, or that some other friend has turned out to be a *jellyfish*, my hearer will understand me just as well as when I say that there is a hairbrush on the dressing-table.

A good piece of advice is 'Don't keep your wishbone where your backbone should be.' This is a little more complex than an ordinary metaphor, for there is also a kind of play upon words in it. It means, of course, 'Do not *wish* for things that you could *achieve* by making a disciplined effort; daydreaming weakens the will to success.' *Backbone* is used metaphorically to imply *courage* and *persistence* (I suppose because our backbone enables us to stand upright and we look more enterprising and bold when we stand upright). *Wishbone*, a part of a chicken, is not usually thought of as a human bone, but here it is used to suggest 'a part of our anatomy with which we daydream'. If we stop to analyse the advice, it is thus somewhat lopsided and illogical; but everyone can understand what is meant at once.

A false analogy may be very misleading. 'Do not criticize the Government; you know how tiresome back-seat drivers are' may sometimes contain some measure of sense, but it is possible to reply, 'If the driver is about to take the car over a precipice, it is reasonable for the passengers to object!' 'You would pluck weeds out of a beautiful garden, so why not remove useless citizens from the country?' sounds very reasonable until we realize that this is going to be an excuse for acts of horrifying cruelty to some human beings. But *all* metaphor is bound to be imperfect; since no two things of different species can resemble one another in every detail, it is possible to point out the limitations of any metaphor, to be flippant by taking it too literally:

> 'Her goodly eyes like sapphires shining bright'
> (SPENSER: *Epithalamion*)

refers to the blueness and the clearness of the lady's eyes; we are not meant to suppose that the eyes are hard stones, or inanimate, or expensive.

When Donne says to his God:

> 'In what torn ship soever I embark,
> That ship shall be my emblem of Thy Ark;'
> (*On the Author's Last Going into Germany*)

we are meant to think of the *protection* of God, of the mercy shown to Noah, of a divine order and plan governing human experiences, perhaps too of an unbroken tradition in the Church—Donne was in later life a priest in the Church of England—but we are certainly not meant to have a picture of the 'animals going in two by two'. Indeed, a large part of the real understanding of metaphor in poetry is our selection of those aspects of the picture that are relevant, and our firm dismissal of possibilities that are not intended to be noticed.

Humorists often point out the irrelevant content of metaphors in order to obtain a comic effect; superficially this

appears to be clever, but if done too often it can create habits
of wanton misreading and spoil poetry for people:

> 'Like a pale flower by some sad maiden cherished,
> And fed with true-love tears, instead of dew. . . .'
>
> (SHELLEY, *Adonais*)

—'Ah!' says our silly-clever humorist, 'but plants will not
grow in a salty soil!'

> 'Those green-robed senators of mighty woods,
> Tall oaks. . . .'
>
> (KEATS: *Hyperion*)

and our humorist says, 'I hope there is no Senator McCarthy
in the forest!' Such *irrelevant images* are to be excluded from
the mind when we read poetry; the poet is entitled to that
courtesy from the reader. He is even, I think, entitled to say
when a reader claims that, for instance,

> 'The pansy at my feet
> Doth the same tale repeat. . . .'
>
> (WORDSWORTH: *Intimations of Immortality*)

suggests to him an effeminate man lying prostrate, 'Well,
that's your fault; I can't help that!' For the poet cannot hope
to produce a metaphor that will carry exactly the same
associations for everyone and that will not in any way bring
in irrelevant possibilities. It is the reader's business to see that
portion of the idea, that resemblance between two unlike
things, that makes the metaphor illuminating; metaphors,
honestly used, as by good poets and orators, are not meant
to save us the trouble of thinking; they are meant to help us
to think more deeply and adequately.

Let us now look at some very well-known lines and
analyse the 'meaning' of the metaphors—a repulsive pro-

cedure, as all dissection of living bodies must be, but, perhaps, illuminating.

> That time of year thou may'st in me behold
> When yellow leaves, or none, or few, do hang
> Upon those boughs which shake against the cold,
> Bare ruined choirs, where late the sweet birds sang.'
> (SHAKESPEARE: *Sonnet LXXIII*)

This means that the writer feels he is old, and implies also that he feels somewhat lonely and broken. Now, the statement, 'I am a poor, lonely old man!' would have a tone of rather unpleasant self-pity and emotional blackmail in a love-poem, which the sonnet is. The metaphor of the tree in autumn first removes the idea one degree from the realm of the embarrassingly personal. There is, of course, one huge imperfection in the metaphor: autumn is merely temporary and every autumn is followed by another spring; old age is a permanent physical deterioration and, at least for the human body on earth, there is no possibility of a new spring. But we must dismiss this association as quite irrelevant to what is now being said; there are huge imperfections in all metaphorical language, just as there are in all other forms of communication.

Additional associations are brought in to stress the aspect of autumn that Shakespeare here intends to emphasize: the *cold*, the *bareness*, the *silence* (absence of bird-song). The *yellow leaves* by itself might suggest too much of colour and beauty, the 'riches' of autumn, so the leaves are described as 'yellow . . . or none . . . or few . . .'. If *gold* or *golden* had been used instead of yellow, the colour adjective would have been equally truthful, but would have brought in agreeable associations such as Shakespeare needed to avoid. The boughs that *shake* may be meant to suggest the tremulousness that is a common weakness of old age. *Cold* carries ideas of loneliness, poverty, deprivation, sexual inability and emotional starvation, as well as winter. The fact that the birds no longer sing on the tree in autumn in itself suggests a deprivation of past joys, a sense of loss, loneliness and melancholy silence; but this is further stressed by the *bare ruined choirs*; and the use of a word that suggests a church helps to suggest also the sanctity of the human being, to suggest that something worthy of sad reverence still clings about the ruin. Lastly, the music of the four lines helps to take away the possibility of unpleasant self-pity and to replace this ugly emotion by a gentle wistfulness that is attractive.

Good metaphorical language may in a sense be far more *truthful* than prosaic non-figurative language; that is the point of writing poetry, perhaps. Responsible users of metaphor are trying to communicate what literal language cannot convey so well.

A fairly common human experience is to wish to do something that in itself seems to us innocent enough, but that would not be appropriate to our situation—that might, for example, discredit our cause or arouse the disapproval of others who cannot understand our point of view. We wish to do the deed, and half decide to do it; why are we being so silly, why restrain ourselves when there is no harm in it?—but then something, call it *conscience*, or *conditioning*, or *inhibition*—at all events it is not a rational reaction—intervenes and we cannot do what we wish. Obviously this may at times be desirable and useful; at other times this inner hindrance may merely be a nuisance and cripple us in desirable activities. At all events, most readers of this book are likely to know the experience.

I have tried to describe the experience in very general and abstract language, as objectively as I can. Here is a politician describing it and applying the experience, not to himself but to others.

'Discipline is what matters; self-discipline' (1). Anyone with any moral sense will know what I mean (2). Anyone who loves his country lives continually under certain restraints (3). We all know this (4). You must all have experienced many times (5) those sacred hesitations, those restraints, those noble refusals, that make a man out of an animal (6). Consider: the temptation comes to you. You are tempted by it (7). But you are a man (8). You cannot even explain why this act is wrong; we cannot always explain the most important and sacred things in life (9). You hesitate; you would very much like to do it; you would so much like just this once, to give up all you stand for, to enjoy yourself (10). Yet something holds you back. Possibly you curse it, possibly you even ask yourself, why am I so silly? But that strange inner force holds you back. You know that if you do not listen to it you will be unhappy (11). You feel it as something sacred, as something more important than satisfaction or happiness (12). And in the end you do not yield to temptation. Yours is the victory' (13).

I do not deny that a man who talks like this may conceivably be sincere. But to the average listener, I think such a portion of a speech has a certain flavour of unctuousness, hypocrisy, unreality. We may briefly look at some of the things that jar:

(1) One of those words that can mean almost anything we want it to mean at the moment.

(2) The implication is the common one in these generalizations: 'no one who disagrees with me has any moral sense'.

(3) Moral blackmail: we dare not question the assertions lest we be supposed not to love our country.

(4) Do we? Perhaps so; but this is flattery of the audience and a further attempt at making dissent or query difficult.

(5) Another trick to render dissent or query difficult. (No one likes to indicate that he may not be 'normal'.)

(6) We have already discussed 'make a man of'!

(7) Of course one is tempted by a temptation; that is what a temptation is for; but for a second this sounds most dramatic and as though something is happening further.

(8) 'Man' as a 'clean word'—what does it really mean?

(9) This appeal to the common inarticulateness of most of us is a kind of flattery of the audience, and also tends to suggest that we have no business to question certain things.

(10) Enjoyment is surely a good thing if it does not do harm to others or to ourselves in the long run. However, most of us have a secret and rather morbid distrust of pleasure (psychologists explain this by reference to what is known as the *super-ego*); and the suggestion that we are capable of something nobler than enjoyment is subtly flattering as well as appealing to our secret fear of pleasure.

(11) Yet now in fact the speaker implies that happiness is to be pursued. . . .

(12) . . . and now, that it is something to be sacrificed. . . .

(13) And 'victory' is a very good dramatic-sounding 'clean word' with which to end the paragraph.

George Herbert, 1593–1633, was a priest in the Church of England and lived a somewhat austere life, thinking this his duty. Sometimes he had impulses of rebellion against his strict mode of life; but some inner voice always called him back to his difficult duty. He writes of this experience in a very figurative poem; the drastically figurative language helps to suggest the violent, emotional thoughts, at times almost chaotic.

THE COLLAR

I struck the board, and cried, No more!
    I will abroad.
What? Shall I ever sigh and pine?
My lines and life as free, free as the road,

Loose as the wind, as large as store.
  Shall I be still in suit?
Have I no harvest but a thorn
To let me blood, and not restore
What I have lost with cordial fruit?
  Sure there was wine
Before my sighs did dry it. There was corn
  Before my tears did drown it.
Is the year only lost to me?
  Have I no bays to crown it?
No flowers, no garlands gay? All blasted?
  All wasted?
Not so, my heart! But there is fruit,
  And thou hast hands.
Recover all thy sigh-blown age
On double pleasures. Leave thy cold dispute
Of what is fit and not. Forsake thy cage,
  Thy rope of sands,
Which petty thoughts have made, and made to thee
  Good cable, to enforce and draw,
And be thy law,
While thou didst wink and wouldst not see.
  Away! Take heed!
  I will abroad.
Call in thy death's head there. Tie up thy fears.
  He that forbears
To suit and serve his need
  Deserves his load.
But as I raved and grew more fierce and wild
  At every word,
Methought I heard one calling, *Child!*
And I replied, *My Lord.*

Sharing neither George Herbert's religious convictions nor

his belief that asceticism is meritorious, I immediately feel a sincerity and a profundity of experience in this poem. The very violence of metaphor helps to suggest the violence and the knotty complexity of the emotion. This poem is in anything but literal language; but it is certainly about something real.

The examination of language in this book has hardly scratched the surface. It is possible to read many books on semantics. It is not possible to learn how to communicate perfectly by means of words, for it is not in the nature of language to communicate perfectly. The reason for studying the meaning of words is that by so doing we may perhaps become a little more honest and communicate a little better. There are many occasions in human life when that 'little' is of great importance to human happiness and morality.

A FEW QUESTIONS

1. To speak of a person as *obedient* or *docile* is usually meant as a term of praise. Can these words ever be legitimately used in dispraise?

2. The expression *just five minutes* has one objective meaning and a number of other personal meanings. Discuss.

3. What do we mean when we speak of a person as a *normal* or *average* person? When are these terms useful and when are they meaningless or misleading?

4. Give ten definitions of *a nice girl* such as might be given by ten different people.

5. What are the various (and numerous) meanings of the word *self*?

6. Explain how the word *protection* has come to have, at times, a sinister meaning.

7. Differentiate the following pairs of words: *lazy, idle; enthusiastic, fanatical; loyal, uncritical; vanity, pride; normal, usual; passionate, emotional.*

8. What motive lies behind the use of such expressions as *the fuller figure, matronly appearance, mature lines*?

9. What is *a great man*?

10. What is the difference between 'I found a large parcel in my room' and 'I found a great parcel in my room'?

11. Make a list of words that you have heard people use as synonyms for *not-agreeing-with-me*.

12. What is the correct meaning of the following words: *psychology, complex* (in psychology), *inhibition, allergic, Bolshevik, romantic, bureaucracy, imperialist*?

How have these words come to be popularly used with inexact and even incorrect significance?

13. Why are *highbrow* and *intellectual* often used as terms of abuse instead, as might be expected, of respect?

14. 'He works hard!' is praise. Why do some people use the word *working-class* in a tone of contempt?

15. What is a *gentleman*? And a *lady*?

16. What is the difference between *weather* and *climate*?

17. Can you account for the totally wrong use of the word *native*, in England, to denote a coloured man? And why are black or brown men *coloured* and English people presumably colourless?

18. Study the numerous metaphorical uses of the word *black*.

19. Examine in as much detail as possible the very numerous and often widely different meanings of the word *common*.

20. What different meanings may be attached to the words *my* and *mine*?

INDEX

Index